The American Nightmare

THE
AMERICAN
NIGHTMARE

SENATOR JOSEPH R. McCARTHY
AND THE
POLITICS OF HATE

ROBERT GOLDSTON

THE BOBBS-MERRILL COMPANY, INC.

INDIANAPOLIS   NEW YORK

For Syma and BG Ebbin

Photos on frontispiece and pages 119, 156, 166, and 172, United Press International Photos.

Photos on pages 19, 80, 83, 91, 99, 104, 112, 115, 158, 160, and 176, Wide World Photos.

B
McC

The Bobbs-Merrill Company, Inc.
Publishers   Indianapolis   New York
Copyright © 1973 by Robert Goldston
Design by Jack Jaget
Printed in the United States of America
ISBN 0-672-51739-X
Library of Congress catalog card number 73-1748
0 9 8 7 6 5 4 3 2 1

Contents

History as a Nightmare

paranoia, n. a mental derangement, especially a chronic
form of insanity characterized by elaborate delusions.

—THORNDYKE-BARNHART DICTIONARY

IN THE UNITED STATES there are a great many people (exactly how
many is not known, but they probably number several million) for
whom the history of their nation since the days of the First World
War has been a continual nightmare. For them, history, which is
nothing more than the record of what men have said, felt and done
during their lifetimes, has the quality of a bad dream, a frightening
dream in which the essential quality is that *things are not what they
seem.* For them the statements or writings of public figures—including commanding generals in the armed forces and presidents of the
United States—are lies; behind the masks which are their public
images they are plotting the destruction of the republic they have
sworn to serve. Historical events ranging from minor local elections
to great wars to the mass movements of hundreds of millions of
people—these have not evolved in a natural and logical manner
but have been engineered for malicious purposes by individuals and
groups dedicated to the destruction of the United States and
traditional American ideals. Behind the history of the recent past
and the ongoing history of daily life there lurks a vast, fearful,
well-organized and cleverly disguised conspiracy that manipulates
words, men and events for its own secret and nefarious ends.

Like all bad dreams, the historical nightmare is composed of
shadows that menace but cannot be grasped; of lurking dangers

that cannot be avoided yet cannot always be named; of hints and suggestions of evil that terrify by their very insubstantiality. But there are moments when the nightmare is broken by a sudden brilliant light that illuminates and exposes the danger. At such brief moments both the shadowy conspiracy and the enemy behind the conspiracy assume solid shapes, drop their masks and are revealed in all their appalling reality.

Who are the enemies thus starkly revealed? They have varied throughout American history. Sometimes they have been Roman Catholics acting as secret agents on behalf of a papal plot to gain control of American institutions and impose the will of the Vatican; sometimes they have been radical labor leaders scheming to lead hordes of workers down the path to bloody revolution; sometimes they have been immigrants seeking to corrupt the United States with foreign customs and ideologies; often they have been small groups of very wealthy men who meet in luxurious boardrooms high above Wall Street, manipulating industry, the banks, the public media, even the government itself, for their selfish private advantage. But since the triumph of the Bolshevik revolution in Russia in 1917, the nightmare conspiracy that has most troubled the sleep of politically paranoid Americans has been the international Communist movement.

It would be understandable if the very real challenge to concepts of individual liberty and economic and political freedom embodied in the power of the Soviet Union, the People's Republic of China and their various client nations supplied the basic fears upon which the nightmare depends. But this is not the case. It is not the strength of Russia's Red Army or the potential of China's numberless millions; neither is it the hydrogen-tipped intercontinental missiles paraded occasionally through Red Square or the blustering of Communist diplomats that provides the source of the nightmare. For these are open and obvious threats against which appropriate defenses may be raised. No, the real source of dread and anxiety behind the nightmare is the deep conviction that one's fellow citizens, one's very friends and neighbors, are either wittingly or unwittingly part of a conspiracy of subversion and sabotage to so undermine American defenses and values that the nation will feebly and perhaps even willingly fall into the clutches of the Communist foe. In other words, the threat lies not in the force of Communist power throughout the world, but rather in the suspicion of plots and treasons at home.

An example of the nightmare school of recent history is to be found in what many millions of Americans still believe to be the ways in which the United States was led into the Second World War. To these people, America's participation in that struggle was the result of a conspiracy hatched between President Franklin D. Roosevelt and British Prime Minister Winston Churchill. Of course Churchill was seeking aid for Britain in her struggle for survival and therefore cannot be blamed for conspiring to mislead the American people; but what were Roosevelt's aims? Was it not true that he led the nation to war only *after* the Soviet Union had been attacked by Nazi Germany? Was it not true that American aid was poured into Russia often at the expense of America's own armed forces? Was it not true that Roosevelt "sold out" American interests at various of his wartime conferences with Soviet leader Joseph Stalin? And, finally, is it not demonstrable that the Soviet Union emerged from the Second World War immensely more powerful than she had entered it? Clearly, Roosevelt's motivation in forcing American entry into the battle against fascism was to help the forces of worldwide communism, not to defend American interests (which were not, in any event, threatened by either fascism or Japanese imperialism). When this conception of reality is challenged by such events as the torpedoing of American merchant and naval ships by German submarines before the outbreak of war, it is suggested that those ships either were torpedoed by British or American submarines acting under Roosevelt's orders or were purposely sent into German-dominated waters to be sunk. When it is pointed out that it was the Japanese navy that started the war with its attack on the U.S. Pacific Fleet at Pearl Harbor on December 7, 1941, the reply is that those planes may well have been American dive bombers and torpedo planes disguised to look like Japanese—again, acting under secret orders from Roosevelt. Or, if not that, then Roosevelt goaded the Japanese into attacking, first assuring himself that the American base was unprepared and undefended—this in order to inflame American opinion. Was Roosevelt then himself a Communist? *Perhaps* not, but *if* not, then he was certainly influenced or even controlled by close associates and high government officials who were either Communists or Communist stooges. Who were these influential traitors? They included many of the nation's leading journalists and clergymen and certain businessmen, as well as the President's personal staff, most of his cabinet leaders, the entire State Department, many powerful senators and congressmen, and most of the higher-ranking generals and admirals of the Joint Chiefs of Staff!

Those who would challenge this utter misconception of recent history, who would point out its total falsity, its complete absurdity, and the absence of the slightest shred of evidence to support it, are themselves suspected of being part of the Great Conspiracy. And this ridiculous interpretation of America's entry into World War II remains today a cherished part of the delusional view of history held by many Americans.

Who are the people in our society troubled by this political paranoia? They may be found in all walks of life, in every section of the country, among every social class and on every rung of the economic ladder. Their names appear on the mailing lists of scores of "hate" sheets—weekly or monthly newsletters attacking this or that race or religious group; they form the membership of such neo-Fascist organizations as the John Birch Society; they attend the political rallies of traditional demagogues such as (in the past) Huey Long, Father Coughlin and Senator Joseph R. McCarthy and (today) Governor George Wallace. They are not conservatives, for conservatives seek precisely to conserve that which is best of America's past. They are radicals who are seeking nontraditional solutions to current problems and who are prepared to abandon basic American laws and ideals in order to achieve those solutions. There is no question of the reality of the fears with which these people are troubled. But it may be observed that their terrors, feelings of persecution and delusions make them easy prey for those who manipulate emotions for personal advantage.

It is not only the political demagogues seeking the advancement of their personal political fortunes who profit from the paranoid nightmares of their fellow citizens; there are also special interest groups representing various commercial interests and the interests of foreign governments who seek, through the manipulation of these delusions, to bring the pressure of public opinion to bear on the government on behalf of policies favorable to their clients.

As has been suggested, political paranoia is not a new phenomenon in the history of the United States, nor is it unique to Americans. And it is important to remember that it springs not only from deeply personal anxieties and feelings of insecurity and inadequacy, but also from objective dislocations brought about by a too rapidly changing world. The transformations in the United States from a rural to an urban, an agrarian to an industrialized, a personal to a mass society have left much human wreckage in their wake: people who for one or another reason have been unable to cope with the bewildering change and complexity and who therefore have opposed the one and simplified the other beyond the limits of reason. It is from among these displaced persons of history that the frightened fanatics of the radical fringe emerge.

These people, though they certainly number in the millions, are (and have been) only a small part of the vast American majority. Because they are few and because they traditionally distrust the political processes of their country, their influence has generally been slight. Yet at times of deep national crisis, in the absence of strong national leadership and in the presence of confusion among the overwhelming majority of politically sane Americans, the views of the paranoid minority make themselves felt.

This book focuses on one of the greatest demagogues this country has ever known. He was powerful because at a time of upheaval and crisis he was able to manipulate the politically paranoid minority to serve his own ends. This he was able to do because he understood—and in some ways embodied—the fears and frustrations of his followers. So significant was his presence on the national scene that he gave his name to an entire era—brief but unforgettable—of recent American history. Yet this man did not make his times but was shaped by them. They were troubled times; times when traditional American values and rights were sacrificed on the altar of political madness; times when American public life seemed to be dominated by betrayal, bullying, ignorance, and—above all—fear. If we can understand some of the basic causes and events, as well as the personalities, that shaped this humiliating and frightened era in our history, we may be better able to sympathetically comprehend the people who lived through it. More than that, we may be able to make sure that history does not, in fact, repeat itself.

CHAPTER ONE

The Junior Senator
from Wisconsin

Communists have the same right to vote as anyone else,
don't they?

—Joseph R. McCarthy

In Washington, D.C., December 3, 1946, was cold and wet; it
promised to be an uneventful day. The autumn congressional
elections were well past, and it would be four weeks before the new
Eightieth Congress convened. The capital's newsmen and the
nervous members of President Harry S Truman's Democratic
administration were looking forward to the organization of the new
Congress with more than a little curiosity; for the first time in more
than twenty years, the Republicans would have a majority. The
international horizon was misty with uncertainty and the gathering
of ominous clouds, but so far only the heat-lightning of increasing
friction between the United States and its wartime ally, the Soviet
Union, illuminated the future. Domestic news was full of the
nation's demobilization after the exertions of World War II;
servicemen returning to seek jobs; industry shifting from wartime to
peacetime production; housing shortages in the major cities; the
problems of war brides; and speculation regarding the war-crimes
trials of high Nazi leaders about to be held in Nuremburg. The
major news story was no longer fresh; it concerned the strike which
United Mine Workers' Union leader John L. Lewis had called
against the nation's coal mines, still operated under a wartime rule
by the United States government. It was partly due to boredom,

7

then, and partly to curiosity that a handful of newspaper reporters assembled in one of the reception rooms of Washington's Hotel Carlton to attend a news conference called by the new Republican senator-elect from Wisconsin, Joseph McCarthy.

The gathered newsmen were confronted by a stockily built man of medium height, conservatively dressed in a dark pin-striped suit. His face was wide and inclined to fleshiness; his eyebrows dark, thick and beetling; his manner open, genial, perhaps even breezy. The senator-elect informed the reporters that he had arrived in Washington only that morning and had immediately telephoned President Truman for an appointment. A White House secretary had suggested that the president might receive him after the new Congress convened, not before. If the president wouldn't listen to him, McCarthy badgered, perhaps the press would. What he had in mind was a solution to the national coal strike. The way to settle it, he declared, was for the government to draft John L. Lewis and his miners into the army. Then, if they continued to strike, they could be court-martialed. "In wartime courts-martial," he added (and the United States was still technically at war), "penalties range up to and including the death sentence."

Some of the reporters grinned incredulously; others stifled yawns. This proposal was certainly unconstitutional, and it wasn't even original. But if they brushed aside the senator-elect's "idea," the reporters were somewhat intrigued by the man himself. Didn't he know that senators-elect, especially those who had never yet served in the Senate, did not demand audience with the President of the United States? Didn't he know they did not call news conferences, but were expected to keep their mouths shut, their eyes open and their ears attentive until they'd learned their new trade? "You're a new man here," one of the reporters remarked. "Why did you call a press conference?" For reply Joseph McCarthy grinned. He knew that his name would be in tomorrow's papers simply for his audacity, if for no other reason. A lot of people would know (never mind why or how) that he had arrived in Washington.

The senator-elect had traveled a long way on the road to the nation's capital, and he had earned most of his fare by his wits. Born on November 14, 1908, on a small farm in northeastern Wisconsin, Joseph Raymond McCarthy was the fifth of the seven children of Timothy and Bridget McCarthy. It was a hard-working, piously Catholic family who struggled to scratch a living from 142 worn-out acres of land about a hundred miles north of Milwaukee near the town of Appleton. Joe was an extremely shy and sensitive boy (he often hid in the barn when visitors called at the white frame McCarthy farmhouse) who feared his stern father and clung to his protective mother. Until he was fourteen he attended a one-room country school; then he went to work on his father's farm. In 1929 (he was just twenty-one) he moved to the nearby town of Manawa, where he found a job as manager of the local store of a grocery chain. Fired with ambition and the superabundant energy that was never to desert him, he went back to school while still managing the store. With the help of a friendly local principal he was able to cram four years of high school into one, and in 1930 he entered Marquette University, a Catholic-run school in Milwaukee. He spent two years studying engineering but then shifted to law. He joined the boxing team (where he earned a reputation as a game if wild slugger) and was elected president of his senior class by one vote—his own, which he had previously pledged to cast for his opponent as a mark of sportsmanship. He was graduated in 1935 and was admitted soon after to the Wisconsin bar.

Lawyer Joseph McCarthy hung out his shingle in the small town of Waupaca near the shores of Lake Winnebago and waited for clients. But northern Wisconsin had never been noted for its prosperity, and 1935 was Great Depression year. Few cases came his way (he handled just four during his time in Waupaca), so Joe supplemented his scanty income by playing poker nightly at a tavern on the outskirts of town. He was a wild player, a bluffer—but lucky. "He was brutal," a friend later recalled. "He'd take all the fun out of the game because he took it too seriously." But this was understandable, since his living partly depended on it. The first signs that Joe McCarthy might have political ambitions surfaced when he joined every civic and fraternal organization in the area, made speeches whenever he could wangle an invitation, and was carefully generous about buying drinks for local business-men and reporters.

McCarthy was an aggressive Democrat during those years of the New Deal under the leadership of President Franklin D. Roosevelt, but in Wisconsin aggressiveness was not necessarily the mark of a liberal. For in that state a third party, the independent Progressive Party founded by Senator Robert M. (Young Bob) La Follette, Jr., had for years taken the leadership in liberal causes and dominated state politics. As president of the Young Democrats for Wisconsin's Seventh District, McCarthy ran for district attorney in the fall of 1936. He defeated his Republican opponent but was swamped by the Progressive candidate.

McCarthy's fortunes took a turn for the better almost immediately, however; he was invited to join the prosperous law firm of Mike G. Eberlein in the nearby town of Shawano. Just why Eberlein hired McCarthy is not known. The older man was a Republican who was ambitious to be elected a Circuit Court judge—perhaps he thought McCarthy's Democratic connections might help him. If so, Eberlein was badly mistaken, for in 1938 his newly hired assistant announced his own candidacy for the judgeship—thereby ending his association with Eberlein's law firm and plunging fully into a political career.

McCarthy's opponent was the incumbent, Judge Edgar V. Werner, a distinguished jurist whose supporters were certain of his reelection. But those supporters had not reckoned with the ferocious energy of the challenger. McCarthy campaigned twenty hours a day all over the circuit district, speaking to farmers, housewives, shopkeepers—anyone who would listen. Although Judge Werner was sixty-six years old, McCarthy continually referred to him as "my seventy-three-year-old opponent" and hinted that the judge was senile. When Judge Werner sought to deny these allegations, McCarthy only advertised them more. Not content with this lie about the judge's age, McCarthy accused his opponent of having "pulled down" $170,000 to $200,000 during his thirty-five years on the bench. This huge sum actually worked out to a modest salary of $4,800 to $5,700 a year, but, as Joe McCarthy knew, few voters would trouble with the arithmetic; only the large figures would stick in their minds. Just before election day, Seventh District voters were deluged with a flood of postcards bearing the slogan "Justice Is Truth in Action," each apparently personally signed by Joseph R. McCarthy. Judge Werner went down to defeat by more than 4,000 votes.

And now began a judicial career truly unique in the history of Wisconsin. It seemed that on Judge Werner's circuit, as on the circuits of all other judges, many cases were backed up awaiting trial in a kind of legal traffic-jam (a judicial trouble still afflicting court systems throughout the United States). The new Judge McCarthy found a remedy for this, however, in his tremendous energy (he kept his court in session until after midnight on many occasions) and his swift decisions (in one instance he granted a divorce in five minutes flat). Within a few months he had adjudicated more than 250 cases awaiting trial on his own calendar and, in accordance with Wisconsin custom, was exchanging circuits with other judges. This gave him an opportunity to travel in all parts of the state. Judge McCarthy soon became a familiar figure to politicians, businessmen and journalists throughout Wisconsin. But while his energy was admirable, the justice dispensed in his court was sometimes questionable, and on at least one occasion, atrocious.

This celebrated incident took place when the state of Wisconsin's Department of Agriculture brought suit against the Quaker Dairy Company to prevent that company from illegally "fixing" and cutting the prices it paid Wisconsin farmers for milk. In an unusual gesture for so speedy a judge, McCarthy granted Quaker Dairy's attorneys a delay of six weeks on the case. Then, when hearings were finally held, he first granted the state's injunction (Quaker Dairy was clearly in violation of the law) and then suddenly reversed himself and dismissed the state's case. Judge McCarthy's grounds for this decision were that the Wisconsin law at question was due to expire in six months. To make Quaker Dairy obey the law would work "undue hardship" on the company. In effect, Judge McCarthy was singlehandedly declaring a state law null and void, further implying that he alone would decide which laws were to be enforced and which were not. Shocked, the Department of Agriculture's attorneys carried the case to the Wisconsin state supreme court. But when that august body demanded the trial records, it was informed by McCarthy that he had ordered parts of them destroyed as being "immaterial." The Wisconsin supreme court delivered a stinging rebuke to Judge McCarthy and ordered him to enforce the original injunction against Quaker Dairy pending a retrial. The judge had no choice but to obey.

This experience might have chastened another judge, but McCarthy was unrepentant. During the retrial he heaped scorn and abuse on the Department of Agriculture's attorneys, blaming them for "all this trouble." He apparently had no concern for the possible consequences to his career, and in this he was proved right. For Judge McCarthy already knew that his future depended not on the views of his fellow lawyers or judges but on the reaction of the voters of Wisconsin. And the voters of Wisconsin, whose basic rights Judge McCarthy had so coolly usurped by his amazing decision, remained indifferent. Neither then nor later was the judge to suffer their disapproval.

Judge McCarthy's motives in the Quaker Dairy case (he may have been influenced by the fact that the company had retained as one of its attorneys a close friend of his, or he may have been bribed) are relatively unimportant as compared to the attitudes his actions revealed. Basically, he very evidently held the law in some contempt; he was prepared to ignore, circumvent or overturn it if it stood in his way. From what personal and social sources did this basic disrespect for law spring? Could it have come partly from the outlook of an older generation of immigrants who brought from their homelands a tradition of law as the enemy and oppressor of the people? Was it partly drawn from the earlier frontier heritage, from the semilawless ways in which pioneers had subdued and exploited a continental wilderness? Did it derive from the traditional suspicion of the "mysterious" law entertained by the poorly educated? Was McCarthy's disrespect for law nurtured by cynicism regarding the basic political processes from which law emerged?

McCarthy's attitude toward the law and toward democratic political processes may well have been shaped by all of these factors; it would also have been reinforced by certain elements of the real social world he had experienced. As a youth he had witnessed the utter breakdown of the Prohibition laws during the 1920s. The government's inability to enforce these laws had given rise to widespread corruption, violence and rampant gangsterism. Later he would have been aware that the law, following the advent of the Great Depression in 1930, had proved itself the enemy of Wisconsin's impoverished farmers when they sought relief—so much so that many thousands of them had taken the law into their own hands, declaring "milk embargoes," defying sheriffs attempting to enforce foreclosure proceedings, and threatening a rural revolution against state and federal authority. Whereas the development of President Franklin D. Roosevelt's New Deal had shown that law could also be the friend and supporter of the dispossessed, it had revealed, through various congressional investigations into the causes of the Great Depression, that many of the nation's top business and industrial figures were criminals themselves. Wasn't the law something the rich evaded and the poor suffered? Wasn't it something gangsters thumbed their noses at? Wasn't the law a commodity bought and sold by politicians? Above all, wasn't it something that you broke if you could get away with it?

Judge McCarthy was confident of "getting away with it," because he knew his attitudes were shared by a very large percentage of the American people (and it would be well to bear this in mind before singling him out for special condemnation). He did not invent these attitudes—he embodied them; if he was able to exploit them successfully it was because he was exploiting part of himself.

The next phase of McCarthy's career was to illustrate how well he embodied certain other traditional American vices, especially the national tendency to exaggeration and the exploitation of "the main chance." For just as the Quaker Dairy case subsided into all-enveloping silence, the United States was plunged into World War II. It took Judge McCarthy just six months to weigh the risks and the potential rewards of military service. As a judge he was automatically immune to the draft; but as a politician he could clearly foresee the advantages that would accrue to a war veteran campaigning in postwar America. It may be instructive to follow his military career in fact and then later in political fancy:

On June 2, 1942, Judge McCarthy applied for a commission in the United States Marine Corps. On August 4, 1942, he was sworn in as a second lieutenant. (*In 1944 McCarthy, referring to himself, would state: "Though automatically deferred from the draft, he left the bench and enlisted as a buck private in the Marine Corps."*) On June 22, 1943, as McCarthy's unit was being shipped across the Pacific, along with others on board the military transport who had never crossed the equator before, he took part in the traditional horseplay of "shellback" initiation. During the "ceremonies" McCarthy fell and fractured his foot. This injury had healed ten weeks later when McCarthy's unit first saw action. (*In 1946, while campaigning for the Senate, McCarthy claimed this injury as a war wound. Once when a heckler asked him why he wore elevator shoes, McCarthy replied, "I'll tell you why I wear these shoes! It's because I carry ten pounds of shrapnel in this leg!"*) McCarthy served as an intelligence officer in the South Pacific, his duties mainly concerned with briefing and debriefing flying personnel. He performed these efficiently and faithfully. At times, for fun but never in combat, he also flew in his squadron's planes, occupying the tailgunner's seat. During these frolicsome flights he would occasionally expend much ammunition firing away at jungle growth and palm trees. His messmates once erected a sign over the base camp recreation area: PROTECT OUR COCONUT TREES. SEND MC CARTHY BACK TO WISCONSIN. (*In 1944, and later in 1946, McCarthy's campaign literature described him as "Tail-Gunner Joe," and he personally claimed to have taken part in 14 or 17 or 30 "dive-bombing missions." Later still, in 1952, when he was a powerful United States senator, McCarthy bullied the Navy Department into awarding him both the Air Medal and the Distinguished Flying Cross for his nonexistent missions.*)

Well now, how many veterans have exaggerated their wartime feats? Isn't such exaggeration so common as to be part of the military tradition? And where, in the old and hallowed American tradition of the tall story, does exaggeration so obscure the facts that truth becomes a lie? Do such exaggerations and even outright lies, aside from devaluing the real sacrifices of authentic heroes, actually harm anybody? That would seem to depend on what uses are made of them—and Joseph McCarthy had very explicit uses in mind.

In mid-1944 one of Wisconsin's Senate seats came up for election. The incumbent was Republican Senator Alexander Wiley, a man of much political experience who was all but certain to win his party's renomination in the primary election and then go on to reelection in the Senate. Not only would it seem brash for "Tail-Gunner Joe" to contest Senator Wiley's popularity both with his own party and with Wisconsin voters in general; it would also be illegal. United States armed services regulations were very specific: no member of the armed forces was permitted to campaign for public office. Not only that, "Tail-Gunner Joe" had never resigned his judgeship (other judges had taken over his duties during his absence), and Wisconsin law forbade circuit court judges to run for any other political office. But again, how much attention did anyone really have to pay to regulations and laws? Joe McCarthy announced his candidacy for the Republican senatorial nomination and managed to wangle a thirty-day leave from the Marine Corps in order to visit Wisconsin. He rushed around the state in his Marine Corps captain's uniform carefully *not* campaigning. Addressing audiences, he always prefaced his remarks with: "I am not allowed to express political opinions for purposes of campaigning, but *if* I were allowed to do so, this is what I'd say. . . ." As for the Wisconsin law prohibiting judges from running for other political office, the state attorney general decided to hold that law in abeyance pending the outcome of the campaign. Although McCarthy polled more than 80,000 votes and ran ahead of two other aspirants for the Republican nomination, he was easily defeated by Senator Wiley in the primary. Evidently, despite the Marine Corps uniform and the carefully cultivated limp with which "Tail-Gunner Joe" enthralled his audiences, Wisconsin Republicans still preferred a political to a military veteran.

But this was not the only lesson McCarthy deduced from the 1944 primary campaign. If he had ever doubted the fact, he must now have been convinced that most people would believe a lie provided it was audacious enough. For no one during the contest had questioned the portrait McCarthy drew of himself as a wounded war hero—even though this portrait was almost his sole claim to the nomination and was totally false. The primary fight also reconfirmed another political lesson—the absolute necessity of an organized political base. It was largely because Senator Wiley enjoyed the support of the Republican State Conference that he had so easily defeated the "maverick" Republican McCarthy. It was not enough to woo voters; an aspiring politician must also win support from the party professionals.

But "Tail-Gunner Joe's" political and military careers could no longer be reconciled. Immediately after his defeat in the primary election, McCarthy applied for a further sixty-day leave from the Marine Corps. When this was not forthcoming, Captain McCarthy resigned his commission. Once again he was Judge McCarthy—

15

and free to advance his political fortunes, that nagging Wisconsin law against judges indulging in politics notwithstanding.

McCarthy prepared to reenter the campaign trail by first developing a two-pronged attack. He joined the Wisconsin Young Republicans Club. This group had long been moribund, all but disregarded by the Republican state machine. But its very hopelessness made it easy to dominate, and under Judge McCarthy's energetic proddings it began to show new signs of life. Under its auspices the judge addressed audiences all over the state; it provided him with that necessary political base. Secondly, he found a means to keep his name before the public—a dangerous means which only a man supremely confident of his ability to gauge the electorate would have dared to use: Judge McCarthy turned his court into the speediest divorce mill in the nation.

To understand the audacity of this, it must be recalled that the state of Wisconsin had been among the first to reform divorce law with a view toward saving marriages. It had created a domestic court system through which county divorce counselors were supposed to patiently explore complaints and then advise estranged couples how they might resolve their differences and preserve their homes. But in Judge McCarthy's court there was no time for this procedure; he issued divorce decrees instantly, with a single rap of his gavel. On one famous occasion the judge began his hearing while still climbing the courthouse steps in company with the wife and the two lawyers of the litigants.

"Are you the lawyer for the plaintiff?" McCarthy asked one of the attorneys.

"I am."

"And are you the lawyer for the respondent?" he asked the other.

"I am."

"Is there anything anyone wants to say before we proceed?" the judge demanded as he hurried into the courtroom. The attorneys shook their heads. McCarthy pulled on his judicial robes, seated himself at the bench and rapped his gavel once. "You are now a free woman," he informed the incredulous wife.

"But is that all there is to it?" she asked. "I thought there would be a court trial."

"We're efficient around here," McCarthy said, grinning. "You wanted a divorce and now you have it."

As the notoriety of Judge McCarthy's divorce mill spread, the Milwaukee *Journal*, an independent newspaper, voiced editorial criticism: "Judge McCarthy," it stated, "whose burning ambition for political advancement is accompanied by an astonishing disregard for things ethical and traditional, is doing serious injury to the judiciary of this state."

But McCarthy had taken the measure of the Wisconsin voters. He believed they would be more amused than scandalized by his "quickie" divorces, and he was a firm believer in another hallowed American canon: any publicity, even bad publicity, is better than none. By 1946 Joseph R. McCarthy had not only developed a secure political base among the Young Republicans of Wisconsin; he was also one of the best-known figures in the state. This was important, because 1946 was another senatorial election year.

At stake was Wisconsin's second seat in the United States Senate—a seat held by one of the most respected members of that body and one of the most formidable politicians in Wisconsin history: Robert M. (Young Bob) La Follette, Jr. Young Bob's father, "Fighting Bob," like all the La Follettes, had been a Republican. But the La Follette brand of Republicanism, reflecting Wisconsin Populist traditions, was liberal and progressive. "Fighting Bob" had fought the trusts, the "eastern bankers," and the "railroad barons" and had taken his "stand at Armageddon" with Theodore Roosevelt in 1912 when Teddy split the Republican Party to form his own Bull Moose Progressive movement. When "Fighting Bob" died in 1925 his sons Philip and Young Bob carried on the family's progressive traditions. During the uninspired reign of big-business Republicanism that spanned the 1920s, the La Follettes could generally be found in opposition to national Republican leadership. Finally, in 1934, after the advent of Franklin D. Roosevelt and the Democratic New Deal, Young Bob founded his own independent Progressive Party in Wisconsin. Under its banners the La Follette brothers (Philip served three terms as governor of Wisconsin; Young Bob was elected four times to the Senate) supported most New Deal legislation and dominated state politics. But by 1946, disagreeing with later New Deal measures and perhaps sensing a turn of the political tides, Young Bob formally disbanded the Wisconsin Progressive Party and tried to lead his followers back into the regular Republican organization. Unfortunately, this political move pleased almost no one. Old-line Progressives were hurt and puzzled; Wisconsin Democrats who had been hoping La Follette would join their party were disappointed; and the conservatives who controlled the Wisconsin GOP were suspicious.

Meanwhile, Joe McCarthy had commenced an all-out campaign to capture the Republican nomination for the Senate. He spoke to audiences all over Wisconsin and whipped his Young Republicans into a frenzy of activity. His intention was to secure the backing of the regular Republican organization. The GOP leadership in Wisconsin would perhaps have preferred a more stable candidate. Aside from McCarthy and La Follette, two other well-known Wisconsin politicians were available. But McCarthy out-campaigned one of them and forced the other to withdraw by threatening to make a front-page issue of his recent divorce. Faced with a choice between the brash north-country judge and the progressive senator, the regular Republican machine in Wisconsin turned to McCarthy.

With the backing of the regular Republican organization thus secured, McCarthy threw himself into the campaign with characteristic energy and recklessness. Again exploiting his "war record," McCarthy urged Wisconsin Republicans to "put a tail-gunner in Congress." He accused La Follette of being a Fascist sympathizer because the senator was lukewarm in his support of the United Nations—and he accused him of being a Communist "fellow traveler" for the same reason! And he accused him of being a "war profiteer" for no reason at all. With considerably more justification, McCarthy charged La Follette with indifference to state affairs. And this was a vulnerable point, for as one of the Senate's "elder statesmen" Young Bob had become so involved in national policy-making that he *had* neglected his own constituency. In fact La Follette did not even bother to campaign against McCarthy until the last two weeks before the primary election. By that time it

That ex-fighting Marine, Judge Joseph R. McCarthy from Appleton, Wisconsin, poses beside one of his modest campaign posters after defeating Robert La Follette in the Wisconsin Republican primary campaign of 1946.

was too late; McCarthy won the Republican nomination by more than 5,000 votes.

But it was none of these factors, important though they were, that brought about Young Bob La Follette's downfall. His defeat turned on the fact that certain of Wisconsin's largest and most influential trade unions were at that time under the domination of Communists. La Follette had earned their undying hatred by making speeches on the Senate floor, warning against the surge of Soviet Russian power across Eastern Europe in 1945. In 1946 he again called for increased vigilance regarding Communist postwar intentions—and stiffened the resolve of Wisconsin Communists to defeat him at any cost. Just enough trade unionists in Wisconsin's industrial centers abandoned La Follette (they entered the Democratic primary instead) to ensure his defeat. Much later, when questioned about the Communist support that won him his nomination, Joe McCarthy uttered the quote with which this chapter opens. But the full irony of the situation would only become apparent later. During 1947 Communist leaders would be driven from Wisconsin trade unions, but by that time they had assured the victory of their own nemesis.

In the general election campaign, McCarthy's Democratic opponent was Howard McMurray, a political science instructor at the University of Wisconsin. But McMurray never had a chance. Wisconsin voters, like voters throughout the nation, were weary, disillusioned and frightened in 1946. After twelve years of the New Deal and nearly four years of war, they were perhaps tired of causes. The reforming zeal of the 1930s had fairly well played out, and the war had exhausted liberal passions. The national Republican leadership played expertly on this weariness with their slogan: "Had enough? Vote Republican!" Public disillusionment and fear had developed from the fact that after all the sacrifices expended in leading the free world to its great victory over fascism during World War II, the United States now found itself menaced by the threat of Soviet Russian expansionism in the new atomic age. Besides, with the death of President Franklin D. Roosevelt in 1945, leadership of the Democratic Party had fallen into the hands of his heir, Harry S Truman, a president by accident and a figure of far less political appeal than his great predecessor.

Candidate McCarthy exploited all these themes. He attacked "the bureaucratic mess" in Washington, the "covered-up scandals" of the Truman administration, the "socialist would-be-dictators" of the New Deal; and he made good use of the national Republican cry that it was "Time for a Change!" He also once again cast himself as "Tail-Gunner Joe," the war hero as opposed to his "civvy" rival, and he even turned his relative ignorance of political science to advantage by grinning shyly and admitting to audiences, "I'm just a farm boy, not a professor." In face-to-face debate with McMurray he often accused his opponent of being "communistically inclined" and "a fellow-traveler." McMurray's indignant denials of these baseless charges only gave them added publicity. But McCarthy's 1946 campaign was not essentially different from those being waged by Republican candidates throughout the country. To the standard appeals and accusations, by 1946 Republicans had begun to add hints of Communist conspiracy to their charges against Democrats; and, like McCarthy, they were finding this an effective political device. In any event, 1946 was a Republican year. For the first time since 1928 the GOP won a national election. The new Eightieth Congress would be Republican, and one of its chief ornaments would be the new junior senator from Wisconsin, Joseph R. McCarthy. He was just thirty-eight.

None of the reporters present at Senator-elect McCarthy's audacious news conference in the Hotel Carlton on December 3, 1946, were aware of the details of his background. But had they been, it is unlikely they would have found anything very unusual about it. And this, in considering the senator's later career, is a salient point to remember. Those who pretend to see in Joe McCarthy's early life anything that would unduly distinguish him from either his fellow congressmen or his fellow Americans are evading some harsh conclusions. Briefly, he was born in humble and rural circumstances; he had earned his own education and become a lawyer; he had entered politics as a Democrat but later switched to the GOP; he had won public office as a circuit court judge; he had served his country in the armed forces; and, finally, he had won election to the United States Senate. Far from finding anything odd about this early career, an honest observer is forced to admit that it is not only common but even traditional as a background to public office.

And if it is argued that the means Joe McCarthy employed to pursue that career were ruthless and at times wholly unethical, then one must ask: How much more unethical were they than the means to success employed by many other politicians and by many Americans in all walks of life? Did he lie at times? Did he threaten and bully at times? Did he skirt both the letter and the spirit of the law at times? Yes; but how many of Joe McCarthy's fellow citizens ever expected to find more virtue in their public officials and elected representatives than they found in themselves? Senator-elect McCarthy had won his Senate seat not because he fooled the majority of the electorate but precisely because his supporters saw in him a very real embodiment of many of their own failings, weaknesses and ambitions. Americans (including the citizens of Wisconsin) have occasionally supported and elected superior men to govern their destinies, men who embodied and appealed to their own best vision of the ideal potential in themselves. But such men are rare, and rarer still has been the public zeal for political virtue and uplift which may raise them to high position. The judgment of reporters who first met McCarthy in Washington on that dismal December day was correct; aside from being a bit brash, as a senator-elect he was profoundly typical.

But of course the reporters were not really very much interested in this new junior senator from Wisconsin, for 1946 was a year of crisis and a year of fundamental change. The reporters had much more important things on their minds.

CHAPTER TWO

The Politics of Shock

> This is a critical period of our national life. The process
> of adapting ourselves to the new concept of our world
> responsibilities is naturally a difficult and painful one.
> The cost is necessarily great.
>
> —HARRY S TRUMAN

AT THE END of the Second World War, once again the United States
faced a problem of national self-identification. Such times of crisis,
when changing realities had forced the American people to new
definitions of their collective will, had occurred often enough in the
past. During the presidency of Andrew Jackson, the republic of the
Founding Fathers had been redefined as a broadly based mass
democracy; during the Civil War a newly enlarged definition of
human freedom had been combined with a new acceptance of the
United States as a centrally governed nation rather than a coalition
of individual states; at the turn of the twentieth century, Americans
had accepted a new definition of their economic structure as
primarily industrial rather than agricultural; during the Great
Depression they had accepted a new definition of their social
structure as urban rather than rural, collectively interdependent
rather than individualistic. And during the 1940s the American
people were forced to abandon their long-cherished self-image of
the country as a securely isolated splendid example to foreign
nations, and to substitute for it a new image of the United States as
the totally committed (and therefore totally embroiled) defender of
democratic-capitalist institutions throughout a complex world.
And, like other crises of national identification, this one was
accompanied by predictable hysteria.

American jitters during 1946, the year that brought Senator-elect McCarthy to Washington, were partly based on objective reality and partly cynically induced by those who saw political advantage in national fear. But before we attempt a detailed diagnosis of the mental health of American society during the immediate postwar years, what was its overall state?

The condition of the American body politic in 1946 was that of a patient who has been granted remission (and hopes it is permanent) from a prolonged, painful and near-fatal disease. The germs of this illness were not unique to America; they had been generated throughout the world by the problems of adapting human society to the industrial-technological revolution of the nineteenth and early twentieth centuries. The symptoms of the malady, which had become acute after World War I, included the centralization of enormous economic power in fewer and fewer hands; the increased helplessness and alienation of individuals in the face of this power; foreign imperialism; and recurrent cycles of domestic depression. Depending on local variations in the disease, certain nations had tried specific remedies. Thus, during the early twenties Russia had established a totalitarian-state capitalism disguised by Communist rhetoric; Italy had embraced the woolly-minded fervors of fascism; and Japan had moved toward militaristic chauvinism. In 1932 Germany swallowed the poison of nazism. England, France, Belgium, Holland and some other nations had managed to preserve their free institutions domestically, but only at the cost of an increasingly brutal exploitation of their overseas empires. The domestic failures and international incompatibility of these several remedies led to the tragedy of World War II.

In the United States the disease became apparent near the turn of the century. By that time the American nation was already the most heavily industrialized on earth. Strikes and protests among industrial workers laboring under intolerable conditions were brutally suppressed by governmental power at the bidding of industrialists and financiers; the political uprising of depressed farmers and rural America embodied in the several crusades of William Jennings Bryan was defeated by bribery, coercion and heavily financed campaigns of fear, later supplemented (in 1898) by the distractions of foreign aggression in a senseless war against

Spain. Both Theodore Roosevelt and Woodrow Wilson identified the cause of the disease as the domination of American society by private concentrations of industrial and financial power. Both presidents (in different ways) had tried to "tame" industrial giantism and private economic domination with the power of government. But Teddy Roosevelt's New Nationalism was defeated when he lost control of the Republican Party in 1912; Wilson's New Freedom became a casualty of World War I. During the 1920s, under the Republican presidencies of Warren G. Harding, Calvin Coolidge and Herbert Hoover, the government, completely dominated by business interests, had not only declared itself helpless to combat the disease; it had unwittingly encouraged its progress. The results were the stock market crash of 1929 and the Great Depression of the 1930s.

The Depression was an experience that traumatized all of American society. The standstill of industry, the breakdown of finance, the seeming hopelessness of the many many millions of unemployed, the coming of "instant poverty" not only to workers, farmers and blacks long used to it, but also to America's middle classes—all of these led many observers to predict either a Communist revolution or a Fascist takeover. Instead the United States suffered the shock of Franklin D. Roosevelt's therapy, the New Deal. Destroying many a vested interest, upsetting many a cherished illusion, the New Deal, guided by the compassion and political expertise of the second Roosevelt, undertook to reform the nation's economic structure and, especially, to regulate private economic power. More than this, the New Deal encouraged the growth of counterbalancing forces to Big Business in the form of big labor unions, government-subsidized farming, and social militancy among depressed minority groups. Through drastic, if pragmatic, measures FDR was able finally to preserve for America both free political institutions and her free-enterprise capitalistic economic system. But although the New Deal with its alphabet of agencies was able to alleviate the harsher symptoms of the Great Depression, it was not able to cure it. The cure was brought about by American participation in World War II—and that long and bloody struggle provided yet another shock to the American body politic.

If American society may be described as convalescent in 1946, it may also be described as apprehensive. The patient's fears were partly self-induced and neurotic; but they were also partly grounded in objective reality. For as Americans looked out upon the world in 1946 there were more than a few very real causes for alarm.

Domestically there was the fear of a relapse into economic depression. The giant war economy had brought unparalleled prosperity to all classes of society. But now the war was over. Though it was true that the long-famished domestic market combined with a potentially vast overseas market might provide the stimulus of a semiwar economy for several years, what would happen after that? Would the permanent structural reforms of the New Deal years suffice to ward off a new depression? No one really knew. Nor did anyone really know what was to be the new role of organized labor (which had come fully into its own only during the war years); or what would be the peacetime results of the wartime migration of millions of blacks from the South to northern big cities; or how well the economy would be able to shift over from wartime to peacetime production; or where jobs were to be found for the fifteen million servicemen and women who were now being rapidly demobilized.

Perhaps of graver import, the international horizon was over-hung with ominous clouds. It seemed that the great sacrifices of the war years had brought not peace but the unsheathing of new swords. China was plunging into civil war between the Nationalists led by Chiang Kai-shek and Communists led by Mao Tse-tung. The first rumblings were being heard from such places as India and Palestine of the storm that would soon bring the disintegration of the British Empire. Britain herself had inexplicably (to Americans) turned her back on her great wartime prime minister, Winston Churchill, and elected an avowedly socialist government. The economies and social structures of the nations of Western Europe had been so ruined by war that it seemed only a matter of time before local Communist parties seized power from the wreckage. True, the United Nations had come into existence, but the veto power accorded permanent members of its Security Council (as a result of American no less than Russian demands) seemed guaranteed to emasculate it. And over all this sifting haze of uncertainty hung the dreadful mushroom cloud of the atomic bomb. The United States had inaugurated the atomic age when it ignited "the light of a thousand suns" over Hiroshima and Nagasaki in August 1945. Although atomic power was still an American monopoly, everyone knew it could not long remain so. The gravity of international problems was now infinitely deepened as mankind developed the means of collective suicide.

The most worrisome of all the aspects of international life in 1946 was the deterioration of American relations with the Soviet Union. As Russian forces, contrary to wartime agreements, brutally imposed Communist regimes on the nations of Eastern Europe, instigated Communist guerrilla movements in such places as Greece and Iran, and increasingly refused to cooperate in the administration of conquered Germany, it seemed that the victors of World War II were already tottering down the road to World War III.

The fears and anxieties arising from all these very real and complicated problems were deeply aggravated for many Americans by both illusion and ignorance.

Perhaps the most widespread and pernicious of American illusions in 1946 was that of unlimited American power. Quite rightly awestruck by their own economic and military accomplishments during World War II, many Americans believed there was an American solution for any international problem. The United States had only to make its wishes known and the rest of the world, through gratitude or fear, would obey. The influential magazines of publisher Henry Luce (*Life*, *Time* and *Fortune*) spoke enthusiastically of the dawning of the "American Century," during which, presumably, the wishes of 145 million Americans would prevail over those of all the other three and one-half billion people in the world. A new Pax Americana would now be imposed—and the people of the world would welcome it, because of course they would recognize that the American way of life was the only sane way. Those who opposed American domination or questioned American motives could only be inspired by evil—and would be dealt with forcefully. Some American spokesmen, especially among the military, were confidently calling for a preventive war against the Soviet Union if necessary. And it was precisely at this point that American illusion met and matched American ignorance.

Ever since the Bolshevik revolution in Russia in 1917, American reactions to most things Soviet had been largely hysterical. Ignorant of Russian conditions, equally misinformed by an irresponsibly anti-Soviet press on the one hand and a small but ardently worshipful handful of American Communists on the other, public opinion in the United States regarding the Soviet Union gyrated wildly between fear and hope, admiration and loathing.

When Lenin and Trotsky led Russia out of the Allied camp during the First World War to make a separate peace with imperial Germany in 1918, Americans, not understanding that Russia had long since been hopelessly defeated and totally exhausted, and that *any* Russian government would have had to give up the struggle, blamed this "great betrayal" on the Bolsheviks. Spurred on by wildly exaggerated press reports of Bolshevik "excesses" and "atrocities" during the admittedly savage civil war that raged in that country from 1918 to 1921, this initial American distrust and disgust prevailed for an entire decade following World War I, during which time the United States refused to so much as recognize the existence of the Soviet government. This blind loathing of the Soviet Union was followed, during the decade of the Great Depression, by growing (but equally baseless) admiration for Russian accomplishments and Soviet policy. Americans noted that the Soviet Union remained unaffected by the Great Depression; they did not see the starving millions of Ukrainian peasants or the slave-labor camps which were the political and social concomitants of a totalitarian economy. Americans also noted that only the Soviet Union seemed ready to "stand up" to expanding world fascism, actively seeking a coalition against Hitler's Germany and directly supporting the Republican side during the Spanish civil war; they did not see the devious ways in which Russian dictator Joseph Stalin's personal neuroses had first paved the way for the advent of nazism in Germany and later betrayed the Spanish Republic into the hands of its Fascist enemies. This growth of American friendship for the Soviet Union during the 1930s was followed by a brief but violent revulsion against Russia when, in 1939, Stalin reversed himself and signed a treaty of alliance with Nazi Germany. When Soviet forces invaded Poland to divide that prostrate land with their Nazi allies, and when in 1940 Russia attacked neighboring Finland, American detestation of the Soviet regime flared to new heights. But once again, after Hitler turned on his erstwhile ally in 1941 and loosed his mechanized hordes against the Russian people, American opinion veered dramatically. The heroic Russian struggle against Nazi Germany evoked boundless admiration among Americans, and when the United States was bombed into the war on December 7, 1941, it evoked boundless gratitude too. Now suddenly Russia was America's most important ally. Americans saw the magnificent way the Soviet government rallied its people to defeat the common enemy; they did not see (or preferred to forget) that the Soviet regime remained an absolute dictatorship. If, in 1946, Americans were increasingly surprised and dismayed at the reemergence of international Communist subversion and national Russian aggressiveness, it was because for nearly thirty years most Americans had not been able to see the Soviet Union realistically.

Between fears (real and imaginary), illusions and ignorance, American society in the years immediately following World War II was particularly susceptible to demagoguery; that is to say, to the conscienceless exploitation of fear and ignorance for political ends. And in 1946 there were not lacking certain individuals and groups in American society willing to carry on a demagogic campaign of terror to achieve their private political and economic ends. This particular campaign had its origins (as we shall see) during the crisis of the Great Depression, but its technique was as old as the republic itself.

Briefly, that technique may be illustrated as follows: Suppose that, for whatever reasons, you are opposed to something—say a piece of pending legislation, a governmental policy, a law or a political party. To make your opposition effective in a democratic society you will have to persuade a sizable portion (not always a majority) of the electorate to adopt your views. Now, if you cannot produce convincing arguments to support your cause, you must appeal not to reason but to fear. The surest way of accomplishing this is to cause the public mind to associate what you are opposed to with something already deemed dreadful by your fellow citizens. In law this method is known as slander; in social pathology as "guilt by association"; in politics as "using a red herring." American history is replete with examples of the successful and unsuccessful use of this technique.

Thus, during the earliest days of the republic, Federalists opposed to Jeffersonian reforms associated their enemies with "seditious elements," implying that all Jeffersonians were bloody-handed agents of the French Revolutionary terror; a few decades later those who feared the spreading of Jacksonian democracy labeled its leader an "atheist," a "radical" and a "murderer." During the 1880s and 1890s, conservatives attempting to stave off industrial reform pictured labor unions as "anarchist conspiracies" and labor leaders as bomb-throwing terrorists. Throughout the 1920s those who opposed progressive social legislation such as child labor laws or minimum wage laws painted these measures as "socialist inspired," their advocates as "Bolsheviks." In every case (and many more could be cited) opposition to progress or reform was mounted not on the lack of merit of a proposal but on an attempt to equate it with something frightful (and preferably foreign) in the public imagination.

The campaign of fear which was gathering momentum in 1946 was actually the rebirth of consciously organized propaganda begun in the early 1930s. Its original aim had been to combat the economic and social legislation proposed by President Franklin D. Roosevelt's New Deal to conquer the Great Depression and rationalize the American economy. To understand the virulence of this campaign it is necessary to recall the circumstances that attended its birth.

All during the 1920s American society was dominated by industrial and business interests. The theme of the decade, sounded by politicians, businessmen and the mass-communications media, was: What's good for business is good for the country. Its inner reality was a feast of prosperity for the rich and for the middle classes based on the exploitation of labor and farmers; its justification was that increased wealth for the few would trickle down to the many and keep everybody happy. Through their absolute control of the reigning Republican Party, big businessmen were able to dictate legislation acceptable to them and to prevent the enactment of laws they deemed injurious. In case after case, federal courts held the rights of property paramount over such "Bolshevik" ideas as preventing the employment of children below the age of twelve or allowing workingmen to bargain collectively. "The chief business of the American people," declared President Calvin Coolidge, "is business." And not only did businessmen enjoy political and economic dominance; their ethics were touted as the noblest ideals of the age. Many years before, President Theodore Roosevelt had described the "typical big-moneyed men of my country" as having "ideals which in their essence are merely those of so many glorified pawnbrokers." But Coolidge (speaking for what was undoubtedly a majority of his fellow citizens) invested them with all but religious significance. "The man who builds a factory builds a temple," declared the president of the United States. "The man who works there worships there." So lofty was the pedestal on which business-men were placed during the decade that advertising man Bruce Barton did not hesitate to declare that Jesus Christ Himself had been "a highly successful businessman." And, looking out at the general prosperity around them, most businessmen were content to accept their status. The ideas, the outlook, the values that had made them rich were justified by the only criterion they themselves accepted: success. Assailed by an overwhelming barrage of probusi-ness propaganda, most of the American people, even including those not invited to the money feast, were inclined to agree.

Then, at the very pinnacle of prosperity, while President Herbert Hoover was assuring the nation that it was "within sight of the day" when poverty would be "forever banished," came disaster. The stock market crash in the autumn of 1929 was followed by a steep descent into the maelstrom of the Great Depression. Within two years, more than fifteen million people were jobless; many millions were homeless; breadlines and soup kitchens, apple-sellers and food riots, shantytowns and bank closures, idle factories and mortgage-foreclosed farms remade the face of America in the image of universal destitution. Despair settled like a pall over the land— along with anger. Just as businessmen had claimed credit for prosperity, so now they had to shoulder the blame for disaster. In actuality, of course, they were responsible for neither, for it soon became apparent that they were no more knowledgeable about what really made the American economy function or not function than any other group. Like laborers, farmers and the now

31

impoverished middle classes, big businessmen and industrialists turned eagerly to the solutions propounded by Franklin D. Roosevelt as the only means at hand for preserving the capitalist system in the United States. They were very willing, in 1932, to turn their political and even economic power over to the New Deal as a simple measure of self-preservation.

But it was not only their power that businessmen lost (or renounced) in 1932; they also lost their standing with the American people as a whole, and even, to a certain extent, their own self-respect. They were toppled from their pedestal, and the fall was painful. Investigations revealed that many big businessmen had engaged in unethical practices; many had been swindlers; almost all were totally ignorant of or totally indifferent to the social results of their mad scramble for money. In stunned fright many industrialists and businessmen awaited a revolution that would make them its first victims.

The revolution never came, of course, largely because Roosevelt's New Deal found speedy, effective and humane if unorthodox methods of alleviating the worst effects of the depression among the masses of the American people. But not only were FDR and his "Brain Trust" eager to feed, house, clothe and find work for the many impoverished millions; they were also determined to effect structural changes in American society that would prevent a recurrence of economic depression. By enacting much of the social legislation that had been bottled up during the 1920s—minimum wage laws, a public power program, and federal aid to agriculture —as well as adopting new legislation such as the Social Security program, the reform of the banking system, and various measures designed to guarantee labor's right to organize, the New Deal encouraged the establishment of new sources of social power to combat the power of business. In the society emerging from all this legislation (which we have no room to examine in detail) the power of business and industry would now be matched by the power of the farmers and of organized labor. And, of even greater significance, it would be matched and overmatched by the power of government. Not only were such hallowed capitalist temples as stock exchanges and banks to be regulated by the government; but, through the workings of dozens of laws, government was to become, in effect, the silent but watchful partner in large-scale private enterprise. Not only that; the government was itself "going into business," especially in the banking and public power fields.

If the Great Depression and FDR's battle against it came as twin shocks to American society, they came as absolutely traumatic experiences to many of the nation's largest and most important industrialists and businessmen. And when the worst of the crisis was past (by 1936) and their worst fears had proved phantoms, many among America's rich and powerful found time to reflect the power that was no longer theirs, the public esteem they no longer enjoyed, and the fact that New Deal legislation threatened permanently to restrict both their former absolute economic freedom and their political influence. In other words, there would be no return to "the good old days" of power for them, no climbing back up onto the pedestal. The gates of paradise were swinging forever shut behind them. It did not matter that the New Deal had saved most of what was essential to the capitalist system, had preserved the free enterprise economy, and in so doing had, in effect, saved the rich from their own worst mistakes; with the political and social blindness that had first occasioned their fall from grace, many, perhaps most, of America's wealthy businessmen and industrialists blamed their condition on Franklin Roosevelt and his "pernicious" administration. FDR himself described the situation during the presidential campaign of 1936 with his usual wit:

"In the summer of 1933," said the president, "a nice old gentleman wearing a silk hat fell off the end of a pier. He was unable to swim. A friend ran down the pier, dived overboard and pulled him out; but the silk hat floated off with the tide. After the old gentleman had been revived he was effusive in his thanks. He praised his friend for saving his life. Today, three years later, the old gentleman is berating his friend because the silk hat was lost."

The rich were not amused. Their party, the Republican Party, was a shambles; the new Democratic coalition put together by FDR—labor, farmers, the urban poor and the minority groups— threatened a permanent political hegemony in America. Furthermore, FDR's buoyant personality, his flair for the dramatic, his persuasive radio voice, his political acumen, and above all his obviously sincere concern for the welfare of the "forgotten man"

33

made him the idol of the vast majority of Americans. Because he could not be successfully attacked personally, and because wealthy businessmen and industrialists could produce no logical argument in opposition to his programs, they turned to the traditional American political technique earlier described as the "red herring method." They opened a large-scale propaganda offensive designed to identify in the public mind all New Deal or liberal measures with communism. They began to paint FDR's closest advisers as secret Bolsheviks and the president himself as a dupe in the hands of sinister Red forces.

Beginning in late 1935 and continuing over the next few years, the political face of America broke out in a rash of extreme right-wing organizations. These leagues, committees and associations had in common their financing (the donations of such tycoons as publisher William Randolph Hearst, Alfred P. Sloan of General Motors, J. Howard Pew of Sun Oil Company, banker Ogden Mills, the I. E. Du Pont family and many others) and their aim: to unseat "that man in the White House."

Listen to the red herring method in action:

Alfred E. Smith (ex-political liberal, ex-Democrat, ex-friend of FDR, ex-"Happy Warrior") addressing more than 2,000 men who, according to the *New York Times*, represented, "either through principals or attorneys, a large portion of the capitalistic wealth of this country" at a Liberty League rally in January 1936: "It's all right with me if they [the New Dealers] want to disguise themselves with Karl Marx or Lenin or any of the rest of that bunch, but I won't stand for allowing them to march under the banner of Jackson or Cleveland. . . . Let me give this solemn warning: there can be only one capital, Washington or Moscow. There can be only one atmosphere of government: the clean, pure, fresh air of free America, or the foul breath of communistic Russia!"

The Republican National Committee in October 1936: "Stalin over in Russia . . . has ordered his following in the United States to back Roosevelt."

William Randolph Hearst (in his syndicated column) in 1938: "The Democratic Party has been captured by the Asiatic philosophies of Marx and Lenin. A few more years of the New Deal and the Red flag will be flying over Washington."

Of this constantly shifting constellation of organizations dedicated to the defense of America against the Red Menace (the Southern Committee to Uphold the Constitution, the Farmers' Independence Council, the Crusaders, the Sentinels of the Republic, the Liberty League, etc.), one was destined to survive to influence events: the Committee for Constitutional Government founded in 1937 by arch-conservative newspaper publisher Frank E. Gannett. Unlike its rival crusaders against the Menace, the CCG worked patiently, diligently and skillfully to organize real grassroots support. It laboriously compiled numerous mailing lists, churned out pamphlets and leaflets by the hundreds of thousands (with such whimsical titles as "While We Go Marxing On"), flooded newsrooms with handouts, set up a chain of radio stations as the Liberty Network, and concentrated on the politics of the possible. That is to say, although the CCG campaigned bitterly against FDR, it recognized the improbability of his defeat and sought smaller victories. The CCG lobbied tirelessly in Washington against specific legislative measures until it grew to be acknowledged as the second most effective lobby (after the National Association of Manufacturers) in the capital. Throughout the country it worked locally for the defeat of liberal candidates (of either party). With generous financing from some of the nation's wealthiest individuals and corporations (including Sears Roebuck, Armco Steel, Kennicott Copper, Republic Steel, Fruehauf Trailers, Champion Spark Plugs, Cities Service Stations, S. S. Kresge, etc.), the CCG could often muster far greater resources in any given congressional district than could the local candidates. The CCG's efforts were further aided by the fact that the conservative owners of America's newspapers (an estimated 80 percent of them) were overwhelmingly opposed to FDR and all his works. Thus CCG "news" handouts were assured wide circulation.

In 1938 Congress, ever sensitive to the winds of criticism, created the Special House Committee on Un-American Activities. Its chairman was an elderly arch-conservative Texas Democrat named Martin Dies. The Dies Committee (as it soon came to be known) pioneered many of the techniques that would one day be labeled "McCarthyism." It made wholesale accusations of Communist infiltration of the government (without ever proving a single one); it

35

declared private citizens to be traitors because they had at some time associated with or been seen in the company of suspected Communists; it welcomed testimony (no matter how obviously self-serving and even perjured) from vengeful or deluded ex-Communists; it bullied "unfriendly" witnesses unmercifully; and, for the purposes of slandering groups and individuals, it did not hesitate to exploit its ties to such sensationalist newspapers as the Hearst and McCormick presses and such self-styled experts on the Menace as columnists George Sokolsky, Fulton Lewis, Jr., and Westbrook Pegler.

Although the committee's title might have led people to believe it would also investigate and expose Fascist and Nazi subversion of the American Way (in 1938 such organizations as the German-American Bund were holding military training exercises to prepare their members to aid the *Wehrmacht* when and if Hitler's hordes invaded the United States), these right-wing threats seemed of little interest to Chairman Dies and his associates. As the nation went to war against fascism, the Dies Committee remained faithful to anticommunism. The reason was simple: the Dies Committee was not interested in either communism or fascism; it was interested primarily in smearing New Dealers and liberals through the ancient red herring method.

During the years of World War II the Dies Committee was relatively somnolent. Its famous chairman resigned from Congress in 1944. But the committee's investigative circuses had grown so popular with many Americans that Congress never failed to renew its mandate and its appropriations.

Yet, after all, until 1945 the red herring method as practiced by the Dies Committee, the CCG and other defenders of 100 percent Americanism was only relatively successful. Despite all the propaganda, the angry editorials, the scare headlines and the money expended, the American people elected Franklin D. Roosevelt four times to the presidency. It was not whipped-up opposition but rather the coming of World War II that brought the New Deal (and the Great Depression itself) to an end. Yet the decade-long smear campaign that had sought to identify reform with Bolshevism and treason was not without its long-term effect. Like the famous ancient Chinese water torture, the steady drip of cynically induced fear on the American public consciousness eventually produced hysteria. And events seemed to conspire perversely to favor the fear-mongers.

FDR died early in 1945, and with him died the tremendous personal charisma and political skill that had forged the New Deal coalition. His successor to the presidency, Harry S Truman, was eventually to demonstrate not a little political sagacity of his own. But in 1945 Vice-President Truman inherited his high office all but totally unprepared for its burdens and powers (he had not even been informed that an atomic bomb was being built), and with the disadvantage of not having won it electorally. The presidential hand that would one day be firm was uncertain at the complex controls of government in 1945. Then, within a few months of FDR's death, World War II ended, and in a few short months the taste of victory was already turning to ashes in the public mouth.

Thus 1946 saw the emergence of many ominous shadows on the American political stage. There was the discouragement and dismay occasioned by all those domestic worries and international disappointments discussed earlier; there was general bewilderment occasioned by ignorance; there was resentment occasioned by illusion—and there were those individuals and groups, still cynically trailing their red herring behind them, who now, for the first time since 1928, sniffed real opportunity.

In January 1946 the directors of the Committee for Constitutional Government established a subsidiary organization called American Action. Its executive director was Merwin K. Hart, long notorious as a rabid anti-Semite and outspoken Fascist. Its funds came from that same old congeries of angry or frightened businessmen (Fruehauf, Weir, the Du Ponts, et al.) who had been bank-rolling extreme right-wing causes for decades. Its techniques and resources were those of the CCG. American Action concentrated on organizing in marginal congressional districts throughout the country (that is, areas where its support might realistically be expected to affect the outcome of an election) and went to work on behalf of the most conservative candidates it could find.

The red herring was never fresher than in American Action propaganda during the fall of 1946. "Leftist minorities terrorize and dictate to Congress and to legislatures!" proclaimed one American

Action leaflet. "Leftists fill many key government posts, local and national. Leftists largely control American movies and the American theater; and, to a larger extent, radio!"

By 1946, so desperate had many Republicans grown after two decades of defeat that even highly "respectable" Republican candidates were willing to echo such nonsense. Thus Senator Robert A. Taft of Ohio, leading spokesman for the Republican Party, charged that the Democratic program "bordered on communism." Ex-presidential candidate Thomas E. Dewey, Republican governor of New York, declared that the Democrats were dominated by "adventurers who owe their allegiance to a foreign ideology." House Republican minority leader Joseph Martin called for the election of a Republican Congress to "sweep the Communists and fellow-travelers from office."

In California a political unknown named Richard M. Nixon campaigned for the congressional seat held by liberal Democratic congressman Jerry Voorhees. With backing from American Action, candidate Nixon flooded the congressional district with leaflets printed on pink paper comparing Congressman Voorhees's voting record with that of avowed pro-Communist Congressman Vito Marcantonio of New York. Of course the fact that Voorhees and Marcantonio had on occasion voted for or against the same measures by no means meant that Voorhees shared Marcantonio's ideology (Voorhees was, in fact, anti-Communist), but the implication conveyed by the "pink sheets" disturbed a sufficient number of voters to give Nixon a comfortable majority on election day.

And in Wisconsin, American Action (with the support of Colonel Robert R. McCormick's influential *Chicago Tribune*) rushed to the support of senatorial candidate Joseph R. McCarthy. American Action financed newspaper advertisements, radio "plugs" and a statewide doorbell-ringing campaign on behalf of this "100 percent American" candidate.

The result of all these efforts was to win the Republican Party control of both houses of the Eightieth Congress. And yet, as has been pointed out, it was not simply the effectiveness of the scare propaganda that overthrew the liberals in 1946; it was rather the combination of many diverse factors. In electing the Eightieth Congress, the American people were registering their increasing fears and worries about the state of the postwar world. Had these not existed it is doubtful that the red herring method would have worked any better in 1946 than it had worked during the previous two decades.

Unfortunately, this most important point was not clearly understood by the defeated Democrats. Without the reassuring hand of FDR at the political controls of their party, they knew only that they had lost control of Congress for the first time since 1928—because, as they supposed, they had been successfully smeared as leftists or as Communist dupes and fellow-travelers. Had they examined the causes of their defeat more rationally they might have been emboldened to meet these slanderous charges head on; perhaps even, as FDR had done in 1936, to turn them to their advantage. But as they straggled back to Congress after the election campaign, the Democrats were too frightened to be rational.

In this they reflected the temper of the American people. Washington, D.C., the capital of the richest and most powerful nation on earth, was a very distraught, very wary and deeply anxious city on that December day when Senator-elect Joe McCarthy held his press conference. Washington suffered from an accumulated legacy of fear.

CHAPTER THREE

The Senator Achieves
Notoriety

The psychopath . . . cannot wait upon the development
of prestige in society; his egoistic ambitions lead him to
leap into headlines by daring performances.

—ROBERT LINDNER

IF THE JUNIOR senator from Wisconsin made but little impression on
the capital's newsmen who attended his first press conference, he
made no greater impression on his fellow legislators when Congress
convened in January 1947 and he was sworn in. But then, first-term
members of the "greatest deliberative body on earth" were traditionally expected to keep their mouths shut, their eyes and ears
open; to treat their elder senatorial colleagues with due deference.

McCarthy treated his colleagues with something more than
deference, for he had an obsessive need to be liked. His was the
heartiness, the open-handed, booming friendliness of the small-town
Elk or Moose; the welcome-wagon spirit of the rural West. He liked
to stalk about the corridors of Congress in his shirtsleeves, exuding
an air of breezy informality. He pounced on first names from the
moment he was introduced to anyone; his handshake was firm, his
smile full of good fellowship. When, as was to happen often in his
career, he felt compelled to denounce his fellow senators in the most
savage and personally offensive ways on the very floor of the Senate,
he would always hasten over to them afterward to clap them on the
shoulder or nudge them in the ribs with a broad, conspiratorial
smile which seemed to say: "Don't take any of this personally. You

40

and I both knew it's just part of the game." And when such advances were met with outrage or rebuff, Joe McCarthy was sincerely bewildered and hurt.

But not all, even of those whom he never attacked, were attracted by his aggressively hearty manner. He was to draw his friends mostly from among those who worked for him and those who, like his Wisconsin sponsors, backed him. But on occasion he could charm an avowed enemy. Richard Rovere, in his book *Senator Joe McCarthy*, recounts the tale of an eminent British journalist who, enraged by some of McCarthy's antics, flew from London to Washington with the avowed and urgent purpose of telling off Tail-Gunner Joe to his face. But after half an hour with the imperviously genial junior senator from Wisconsin, the British journalist had to confess that, much as he detested McCarthyism, he could not bring himself to detest McCarthy.

Joe McCarthy's private vices (that is to say, those he did not practice in public) were evidently few and fairly typical. As a longtime bachelor he had a decided eye for the ladies; he also had a deep thirst for liquor (which did not, however, border on alcoholism until near the end of his career). Aside from this he enjoyed gambling on the stock market and playing high-stake poker (always bluffing on the poor hands). His enemies (and he would have many before he was through) spent much time and effort attempting to dig up evidence of more sinister personal failings but were unsuccessful.

Above all, Joe McCarthy liked to create about himself an aura of importance. Whatever he was immediately interested in he invested with tremendous significance—a significance generally out of all proportion to its real importance. Thus, later, a "pink" army dentist was to be presented to the nation as a top Soviet secret agent whose nefarious activities endangered the very life of the republic; governmental filing clerks were transformed into "top State Department policy-makers," etc. And when McCarthy was not immediately engaged on any particular topic, he would give winks, significant glances, and mysterious hints, all calculated to convince an onlooker that although he could say nothing at the moment, he was embarked upon a fateful mission of the most profound importance.

When faced, as he sometimes was, by people who would denounce him in no uncertain terms, McCarthy retreated. He failed to show up for more than a few confrontations with enraged and aggressive victims. And his eyes had a way of shifting before the steady gaze of an accuser. Many attributed this to cowardice, and perhaps they were partly right. But among those who knew McCarthy best, it was sometimes suggested that Joe simply could not stand outright hostility. He was not only the little boy shouting, "Hey, look at me!" He was also the little boy whose desire to be liked and admired verged on the psychotic. Certainly, from the moment he entered the Senate chamber, he seemed determined, one way or another, to "make his mark" on that body.

As a freshman, McCarthy was assigned to sit on the Senate Committee on Banking and Currency and on the Committee on Expenditures in the Executive Departments. Neither of these assignments at first interested him much. His voting record soon made apparent the fact that he was an arch-conservative on domestic matters (he opposed continued price control, sugar rationing, public housing, and federal aid to education while supporting tax reduction and the Taft-Hartley anti-union labor legislation) but an internationalist in foreign affairs (he supported aid to Greece and Turkey, various aspects of the United Nations, and later even the Marshall Plan). He also worked diligently on behalf of various special-interest groups in Wisconsin and concerned himself mildly with veterans' affairs. In all of this there was nothing unusual or notable. Yet within a few months of taking his Senate seat, Joe McCarthy was well on his way to earning an unsavory reputation among his colleagues.

To appreciate the impact made by the Senate's "remarkable upstart" (as Joe McCarthy was soon to be called) upon that august body, it is necessary to understand something of senatorial folkways. The upper house of the United States Congress is, for a political arena, a notably decorous and somnolent chamber. Tempers are very rarely lost, and then only during the most bitter debates. The crushing personal insults, the shouting matches and the vulgar clamor often heard in England's House of Commons (as well as the wit displayed) are unknown to its American heir. The passion and general hysteria that often enliven the proceedings of France's

Chamber of Deputies would be equally unimaginable on the Senate floor. The days when senators, reflecting the vigor of a youthful nation, fell upon each other with fists when invective failed are long past; the spectacle of the Honorable Member from North Carolina ("Bully" Brooks) savagely beating the Honorable Member from Massachusetts (Charles Sumner) into insensibility in the Senate aisle with a gilded cane are but a distant memory. Senators generally refrain from impeaching each other's political motives just as they refrain from impugning each other's personal honor. The atmosphere prevailing in the Senate is that of a very genteel and exclusive private club.

There are several sufficiently good reasons for the tact with which the assembled Senate conducts its affairs. First of all, almost all important Senate business is discussed and decided in various committees long before its substance is debated on the floor. Senators commonly reach agreement for or against proposed legislation in their committee hearing rooms, their caucus rooms, the halls, cloakrooms and even the lavatories of the Senate before assembling to record their votes. The animosity, passion and bile are generally expended during these decisive preliminary pro-ceedings, with little left over to mar the course of public debate. Speeches made in the Senate are most often designed not to influence the already settled opinions of fellow members but to express "for the record" those views which the senators hope will win them renewed favor with their constituents. Such performances are not calculated to arouse much interest, let alone anger.

Nor is it profitable for senators to belabor each other even if they so desire. Each is elected for six years from widely separated and very powerful private political satrapies. Hence they are all but immune to attacks from their colleagues. The voters of Utah, for example, will hardly be influenced in their support for one of their senators by an attack upon him made by, say, a senator from Florida. Thus inter-senatorial bellicosity is generally a waste of breath.

Of course senators may always empty the vials of their wrath on the executive branch of the government; but since the president, cabinet members and various other executive officials (unlike their English and French counterparts) do not personally sit in the

Congress to advocate their policies or defend their actions, they make somewhat remote targets.

Finally, of course, it must be remembered that beneath the decorous surface of its public proceedings, the Senate remains a battleground for powerful interests and ambitious men. Its self-imposed rules, both written and unwritten, concerning such delicate matters as seniority, reciprocity and courtesy are designed to make possible the orderly resolution of important issues. Though these rules and customs may be criticized for such practices as favoring age over merit and, on occasion, fostering ambiguous "deals" at public expense, without them the Senate could not transact its legislative business. A senator who fails to adhere to these customs or who brings them into disrepute is quickly ostracized by his fellows.

To learn the intricacies of senatorial custom requires time and patience; to practice them requires tact and a willingness to compromise. But the junior senator from Wisconsin displayed neither of these qualities. Illustrative of the matters with which he busied himself during his early years in the Senate and the methods he used to advance his interests was the affair which earned for him among the capital's newsmen the nickname, "The Pepsi-Cola Kid."

During the war, and extending into the immediate postwar years, there was a scarcity of many commodities which as a result, in the public interest, had to be rationed. One such commodity was sugar, which was in especially short supply during 1946. Housewives wanted more sugar for home canning, and industry wanted more sugar in order to produce, among other things, soft drinks. It was certain that if sugar rationing was ended, industry would gobble up all the sugar available, leaving little or none for private consumption. Particularly interested in raising the sugar-rationing quotas was the Pepsi-Cola corporation, at that time engaged in a desperate sales contest with its great rival, the Coca-Cola corporation. Lobbyists representing the Pepsi-Cola interests besieged the Department of Agriculture and busily sought congressional support. They were instrumental in getting before the Senate a measure to end sugar rationing. It so happened that Wisconsin beet-sugar producers were equally anxious to see an end to irksome controls on sugar production (which would mean higher prices for their product). In searching for a suitable champion to lead the anti-rationing forces in the Senate, the Pepsi-Cola lobbyists settled unerringly on Wisconsin's Joe McCarthy. Soon the senator was being entertained at lunches and dinners by Pepsi-Cola president Walter Mack; he found himself spending festive weekends with Pepsi-Cola lobbyist Russell M. Arundel. Indeed, so quickly did the Arundel-McCarthy friendship ripen that when the senator mentioned to the lobbyist that he was in some financial difficulty (he owed a Wisconsin bank more than $169,000), Arundel generously endorsed McCarthy's personal note in the amount of $20,000.

These small favors (combined with McCarthy's legitimate if not very public-spirited advocacy of the interests of Wisconsin sugar producers) were not without their effect. The senator made himself the leader of the anti-rationing forces in Congress. On March 27, 1947, Senator McCarthy told his colleagues that his own calculations revealed that the United States was in possession of "791,000 tons of sugar upon which we had not counted." With so much additional sugar available there was no need for further rationing.

While the Senate listened respectfully to these remarks, not all senators were convinced of their accuracy. One of the doubters was Senator Charles W. Tobey, a New Hampshire Republican who had the interests of the home-canning housewives of his state very much at heart. He warily rose to point out that McCarthy was arguing on behalf of industrial sugar consumers and ignoring the interests of the nation's housewives.

Not so, replied McCarthy; there was sugar enough and to spare for everyone. "Within the past ten minutes," he asserted, "I have received word from the Department of Agriculture that they . . . wish to discuss with us the possibility of agreeing to make available during . . . the canning season, a total allotment of 20 pounds of sugar [per housewife] . . ."

Unable to believe in the sudden largess of the Department of Agriculture, Senator Tobey quietly slipped away from the Senate floor to telephone Secretary of Agriculture Clinton P. Anderson. When he returned, the New Hampshire senator was quivering with righteous indignation.

"The Department of Agriculture's announced position," Tobey

told the Senate, "was misrepresented by the senator from Wisconsin today. Here is the answer which came from Secretary Anderson just three minutes ago, over the telephone, to me: 'I authorize you to state that I have not at any time made a statement that we can give more sugar for home consumption now. . . . There is no more sugar available for home consumption. . . .' That is Secretary Anderson's statement, and it refutes the statement which has been made by the senator from Wisconsin."

McCarthy jumped to his feet and roared: "I don't give a tinker's damn what Secretary Anderson says about the matter. The sugar is here!"

Senator Tobey continued grimly: "On the question of veracity I would not choose between the two gentlemen, but on a question of fact, I take the Secretary of Agriculture any time."

Stung, McCarthy lashed back recklessly. He accused Senator Tobey of having told him privately that he intended to ". . . do nothing more or less than deceive the housewife."

Tobey was outraged. "I take exception to his derogatory remarks," he cried. "The senator's statement, I submit, far contravenes the truth, to put it plainly. . . ."

McCarthy attempted to interrupt, but Tobey went on relentlessly.

"I am not quite through yet, sir. I point out that the senator is confusing the Senate of the United States by a heterogeneous mass of figures which will not stand the test of accuracy. . . ."

Eventually sugar rationing was reimposed, but only after McCarthy had won an amendment to the act which terminated all controls five months earlier than the government wished.

In all of this, what was essentially uncommon was not McCarthy's support of private as opposed to public interests (more than a few senators joined him in emasculating the sugar rationing act), nor was it the fact that he had accepted personal favors from the sugar lobby (senators before and since McCarthy have been known to accept such bribes from various private groups); what was unusual was McCarthy's behavior in the Senate. He had, not to put too fine a point on it, lied to his colleagues in such a blatant and simple-minded way as to insult their intelligence. And, when challenged, he had made a false accusation against his opponent—

an accusation calculated to undermine his opponent's relations with his own constituents. Such behavior was frowned upon in the "club".

Having won the nickname "The Pepsi-Cola Kid" in his first legislative foray, Wisconsin's freshman senator next set about earning himself the title "Water-Boy for the Real Estate Lobby." In 1946 the United States was suffering from a severe housing shortage. Home and apartment-building construction had slumped badly during the decade of the Great Depression and had been brought to a complete halt by the materials shortage of World War II. In the meantime the nation's population had increased, and now to this "normal" backlog of demand for new housing were added the desperate requirements of many millions of returning service-men with new families but no homes. There was a widespread demand for government-sponsored public housing to meet this crisis. Only government help, it was felt, could provide sufficient housing at rental prices that the poor and a large percentage of the returning veterans could afford. So great was the need and so obvious the solution that even such arch-conservatives as Ohio's Republican Senator Robert A. Taft favored a government public housing program. In fact Taft allied himself with liberal Demo-cratic Senators Robert Wagner of New York and Allen Ellender of Louisiana in sponsoring an omnibus housing bill that included a public housing provision.

Opposition to public housing centered, of course, around private homebuilders, private manufacturers of prefabricated dwellings, construction companies, land speculators and real estate groups. All of these smelled the fat profits to be made from the housing shortage—and they wanted no government interference with their exploitation of the country's desperate need. As they marshaled their forces to campaign against public housing, the real estate lobbyists (who would eventually spend more than $300,000 to influence Congress) settled, as had the sugar lobbyists before them, on Senator Joseph R. McCarthy to lead their attack. The senator already enjoyed close connections with several wealthy individuals interested in the private manufacture and sale of homes, especially prefabricated dwellings. These individuals included Walter Har-nischfeger, a Milwaukee industrialist who had generously supported McCarthy's senatorial campaign in Wisconsin; William J. Levitt, the originator of the "Levitt House," whose speculations would soon blossom into Levittowns on Long Island and in Pennsylvania; and Carl Stranlund, president of the ill-fated Lustron Corporation which proposed to build millions of porcelain and aluminum prefabricated houses but which, after borrowing more than $35 million from the U.S. government, went bankrupt without having built anything. A Senate investigating committee later discovered that Lustron President Stranlund was in the habit of cashing checks for Senator McCarthy at the racetrack—to make up any losses the senator may have suffered during the day—and then courteously tearing up the checks. The Lustron Corporation also generously paid Senator McCarthy $10,000 for a seven-thousand-word essay on the virtues of prefabricated houses which was incorporated into a sales brochure for the corporation.

In return for the friendly favors showered upon him by these people and by Washington's powerful real estate lobby, Senator McCarthy undertook to lead the battle against "socialistic and un-American" public housing proposals. In doing so the junior senator from Wisconsin was pitting himself against some of the wiliest and most experienced men in Congress. But he proved equal to the contest.

In the summer of 1947, in order to consider the merits of the Taft-Wagner-Ellender Housing Bill and to hold public hearings on it, Congress established a joint Senate-House Committee on Housing. Senator McCarthy was appointed to this committee, the majority of whose members were public housing advocates. It so happened that through the rules of seniority, chairmanship of the committee should have devolved upon McCarthy's old foe, Senator Tobey of New Hampshire. But when the committee held its organizational meeting on August 19, 1947, McCarthy took advantage of a procedural loophole to deny Tobey the chairmanship.

This loophole revolved around another ancient senatorial custom: a senator who is absent from a committee meeting may cast his votes by proxy; another senator may cast them on his behalf. Thus when Senator Tobey entered the committee room, although he found that of the nine members present, five were opponents of public housing, he was not particularly worried because he personally held the proxies of four pro-public housing members who were absent. These, combined with his own vote and those of the pro-public housing members actually present, provided a comfortable majority. But while Senate rules allow the use of proxies, House rules do not—and this was a joint Senate-House committee. Senator McCarthy quickly proposed that the committee accept no proxies, that only the votes of those present be counted.

This was an outrageous suggestion. Senator Tobey angrily pointed out that in all his long experience the voting of proxies in committees (including joint committees) had never been questioned. Another member present, Democratic Representative Wright Patman of Texas, stated that in all his twenty years in Congress the wishes of absentee members, as expressed through their proxies, had always been respected. "We are all gentlemen here, aren't we?" he asked.

Unfortunately the answer was no. By a five-to-four vote the committee decided not to accept proxies. By the same vote the anti-public housing minority of the committee was able to seize full control. Chairmanship of the committee was awarded to New York Representative Ralph Gamble, who soon proved himself to be a vacuous mouthpiece for the vice-chairman, none other than Joseph R. McCarthy. Between them, Gamble and McCarthy saw to it that the committee's hired investigative staff was drawn exclusively from the ranks of the real estate lobby.

The Joint Committee on Housing, now completely dominated by McCarthy, spent the remainder of 1947 and the early months of 1948 touring the country, listening to any and every citizen who wished to testify on the subject of housing. To amass a preponderance of anti-public housing testimony, McCarthy resorted to a few simple procedures. He always made sure that spokesmen for private manufacturers, real estate groups and construction companies— that is to say, the bitterest foes of public housing—testified first and testified at extraordinary length. By the time they had finished, it often transpired that there was simply no time left to hear the testimony of those in favor of public housing. And when there was time, such advocates (generally mayors of cities, leaders of local civic organizations, spokesmen for veterans' groups) found themselves bullied and harassed by Vice-Chairman McCarthy, whose constant interruptions and irrelevant questions soon ensnarled their testimony in petty discrepancies and fruitless arguments over meaningless detail.

When the hearings ended, the committee staff (composed, it will be recalled, of agents of the real estate lobby) prepared a six-thousand-page report so lopsidedly falsified in favor of the enemies of public housing that the full committee, now regaining control under the leadership of Senator Tobey, rejected the report and caused their own to be printed. Despite the fact that this "Tobey report" was the official statement of the committee (it favored public housing and urged support for the Taft-Wagner-Ellender bill), McCarthy had the original rejected report printed at government expense and distributed as if *it* were the committee's final word on the subject.

When Senate debate opened on the Taft-Wagner-Ellender Housing Act, McCarthy continued his confusionist tactics. His voice, loudly bawling misleading statistics, irrelevant questions and accusations of "socialistic legislation," seemed to dominate the proceedings. Only by exerting all his potential skills was Senator Taft able on April 22, 1948, to win Senate approval of his housing act. This, however, proved but a hollow victory. Taking their cue from McCarthy's rantings, a majority of the leaders of the House of Representatives refused to accept the act until it had been stripped of its public housing provisions. After months of wrangling, Senator Taft finally surrendered, allowing the passage of a McCarthy-drafted substitute housing bill which effectively killed any hope of public housing. This measure, as Senator Tobey bitterly commented, was calculated only to "benefit the builders and those wealthy and moderately well-to-do who can afford to buy their own homes." Mayor Francis H. Wendt of Racine, Wisconsin, put it more bluntly when he declared: "The homeless people of Wisconsin can thank McCarthy for keeping them homeless."

By the time the Eightieth Congress adjourned in the late summer of 1948, the junior senator from Wisconsin had made himself a host of powerful enemies and a reputation as a "troublemaker." He had also helped to paralyze Senate action on some much-needed legislation, thereby handing political ammunition to President

Harry Truman and the congressional Democrats, who campaigned that autumn so effectively on the theme of the "do-nothing Eightieth Congress" that they rewon control of both the Senate and the House of Representatives. When the Eighty-first Congress convened (organized now by its Democratic majority) in January 1949, Senator McCarthy could count on few friends in the Senate. He was dropped from all his committee assignments by the Senate Democratic leadership with the full approval of Senate Republicans. The only position he was now allowed was a seat on the lowliest and most unimportant of Senate committees, the Committee on the District of Columbia. Furthermore, he found that when he rose in the Senate to speak on a measure, his colleagues had a way of ignoring him; when he proposed amendments to pending legislation, he found them rejected summarily. The Senate was protecting itself from its "bad boy" simply by excluding him from its deliberations and proceedings. Yet this very exclusion goaded McCarthy into the third and most famous of all his early political adventures, one that was to win him national notoriety.

The affair that was to provide new fuel for Senator McCarthy's sputtering career grew out of one of the Second World War's more bestial episodes. In December 1944, out of the snow-covered and mist-laden forests east of the Belgian frontier, the last great German offensive of the war crashed into the Allied lines. At first modestly successful in what would one day be known as the Battle of the Bulge, *Wehrmacht* forces advanced against surprised and disorganized American resistance. Partly in a mood of savage jubilation at their unexpected gains, partly in vengeance for past defeats, and partly because they had been ordered to display the utmost brutality, German troops shot down hundreds of unarmed Belgian civilians and captured American prisoners of war as they advanced. Near the town of Malmedy, Belgium, men of the German First SS Panzer Division marched 150 captured GIs into a wheatfield and slaughtered them with machine-gun fire.

After the war seventy-three SS soldiers were tried by an American war-crimes tribunal and convicted of participation in the "Malmedy Massacre." Forty-three of the guilty were sentenced to death. Subsequently all the cases were reviewed by both the War Crimes Review Board and the Office of the Judge Advocate, and a number of the sentences were reduced or dismisssed. In the immediate aftermath of the war, with Nazi barbarities fresh in their minds, the public in general felt that the treatment of these SS murderers was, if anything, too lenient.

But by 1948 American memories had become somewhat dimmed and American interests had changed. With the beginning of the Cold War between the United States and the Soviet Union, it was felt that Germany—especially German industry—must play a crucial role on the American side in rebuilding the shattered economic strength of Western Europe. To win this support it seemed expedient to placate German public opinion. Sensing the possibilities inherent in this change of atmosphere, the German SS defendants in the Malmedy case petitioned the United States Supreme Court to overturn their convictions. Their lawyers presented (for the first time) a collection of affidavits charging that the American prosecutors had used torture and intimidation to extract confessions from them. The Supreme Court refused to hear the petition on the grounds that it had no jurisdiction in the matter. But a publicity campaign (instigated and conducted, as it later appeared, by Soviet agents) had begun to stir German sympathies for the "victimized" SS men. As a means of allaying German suspicion, two new investigations of the matter were undertaken. One of these was conducted by the Office of the Judge Advocate, the other by a special judicial panel headed by Judge Gordon Simpson of the Texas Supreme Court. Both investigations found that although the American prosecutors of the SS troopers had employed a wide variety of psychological tricks to extract confessions, they had not used any kind of torture or physical violence. Nonetheless, in view of certain procedural irregularities, the twelve death sentences still pending from the Malmedy case were commuted to terms of life imprisonment. One would have thought this display of clemency would have ended the matter. That it did not may be charged to the unfortunate circumstance that one of the members of the Simpson panel was Judge Edward L. Van Roden of the Orphan's Court of Delaware. Judge Van Roden, whose sympathies were extremely pro-German (and who publicly endorsed various pro-Fascist and anti-Semitic views) returned to the United States after the panel's investigative mission in Germany to publicly accuse the American Malmedy prosecutors of all sorts of heinous crimes. Later this pro-Nazi judge was to repudiate his statements, point by painful point, before a Senate investigating committee—but that was long after his intemperate outbursts had stirred American uneasiness.

By April 1949, public interest in the Malmedy case had grown so intense that the Senate felt constrained to look into the matter. Accordingly, a special three-member subcommittee of the Senate Armed Services Committee was appointed to investigate the entire affair. Chairman of this subcommittee was Connecticut's mild-mannered Republican Senator Raymond E. Baldwin. His fellow members were Democratic Senators Estes Kefauver of Tennessee and Lester C. Hunt of Wyoming. Permitted to sit in at the subcommittee hearings (a routine courtesy) was Senator Joseph R. McCarthy.

There were several reasons why McCarthy might have wanted to associate himself with this investigation. For one thing, he was undoubtedly influenced by the fact that Wisconsin had a large German-American population; his constituents would follow the proceedings with more than average interest. For another, as noted before, his conduct in the Senate had caused his colleagues to more or less exclude him from the legislative process; they would find it less easy to exclude him from the investigative process. Then, perhaps of greatest importance, there was the fact that one of McCarthy's closest friends, most powerful supporters and generous financial angels was Wisconsin industrialist Walter Harnischfeger.

Harnischfeger, it will be recalled, had been interested in blocking public housing so as to maintain a more lucrative market for his own prefabricated dwellings. He was also deeply interested in German-American relations and had long been known as an ardent admirer of Adolf Hitler (he had distributed autographed copies of der Fuehrer's gospel Mein Kampf and little enamel swastikas to close friends). During the war, while the Harnischfeger Corporation was being cited by the U.S. government for discriminating against Jews and blacks, its president was advocating a negotiated peace with the Nazis. After the war, Harnishchfeger busied himself with various German relief societies. Through the Malmedy hearings Harnischfeger, of course, hoped to vindicate both the conduct of the

Nazis and his own personal views. So eager was he to exploit this opportunity that he sent one of his own "bright" young men, Tom Korb, to act as McCarthy's "administrative assistant" during the committee hearings.

Senator Baldwin and his fellow subcommittee members had as one of their primary purposes the defense of the U.S. Army against what they considered outrageous slanders. Guest Senator McCarthy's purpose was just the opposite. And the makeup of the subcommittee permitted McCarthy a field day. Senator Kefauver was generally absent from the hearings; Senator Hunt was generally silent; and Chairman Baldwin was excessively hesitant, because he had been charged (by McCarthy) of having a personal interest in the proceedings, since one of the American Malmedy prosecutors had been a member of Baldwin's private law firm. Under these circumstances McCarthy all but took over the hearings. He showed himself a master at the construction of hypothetical questions deliberately designed to cloud the issue and of self-accusatory questions of the "When did you stop beating your wife?" variety. He did not hesitate to imply that the Malmedy prosecutions had been "vengeance trials" because some of the American investigators and prosecutors were Jews. He constantly interrupted witnesses, attempting to confuse them, and tried to bully those he could not confuse. He shouted that the attitude of the secretary of the army was "fantastic," that a statement by the judge advocate general was "the most phenomenal I've ever heard," that the American military judges were "morons," that army witnesses (including some survivors of the massacre) were "lying." He accused the subcommittee members and their investigative staffs of attempting to "whitewash" the U.S. Army. In a final dramatic outburst he demanded that all the American Malmedy investigators, prosecutors and judges be forced to submit to lie-detector tests. When the full Senate Armed Services Committee contemptuously rejected this demand (as McCarthy knew they would—lie-detector evidence is not accepted in American legal procedures), the Wisconsin senator stalked out of the hearings charging that they were "phony."

Just as McCarthy's rough-handed tactics dominated the subcommittee chamber, so his name dominated press reports. "McCarthy

SCORES BRUTALITY!" "McCARTHY CHARGES WHITEWASH!" "McCARTHY ACCUSES ARMY!" screamed the headlines. If ever Joe McCarthy had wondered how to generate publicity, he now knew. There were but few headlines to be wrung from the legislative process, the tedious grind of lawmaking with its small victories and constant compromises. Headlines were to be won through the investigative process; and the rougher the investigation, the more dramatic its conduct, the more reckless its charges, the larger would be its portion of publicity.

Two months after he had stormed out of the hearings of the subcommittee, McCarthy took the Senate floor to denounce its members. He accused Senator Baldwin of being "criminally responsible" for a serious miscarriage of justice. In the face of this savage attack the full Senate Armed Services Committee felt compelled to take the unusual step of passing a resolution expressing their confidence in Baldwin's integrity and his handling of the hearings. Despite this public rebuke to his tormentor, and despite the fact that the Senate accepted his subcommittee's findings (which completely exonerated the U.S. Army), the Connecticut senator found he could no longer stomach his job. With men like McCarthy roaring on the Senate floor, Senator Baldwin preferred to retire—and so he did, in the middle of his term, to accept an appointment to the Connecticut Supreme Court. He thus became the first—but not the last—senatorial victim of McCarthy's tactics.

Thus, as 1949 drew to a close, the junior senator from Wisconsin had made himself into something of a senatorial scandal. Politically he had earned the loathing of the leadership of both parties in the Senate, such powerful men as Democrats Lyndon Johnson, Millard Tydings and Richard Russell; Republicans Styles Bridges, Leverett Saltonstall and William Knowland. On a personal level he could find few friends among his colleagues. Even those who might have responded to his excessively hearty, back-slapping, coarse personal manner were repelled by his recklessness and the odor of graft that clung to him. He had broken all the rules of the "club," and broken them with apparent indifference to the consequences. In this he differed from such predecessors as Huey Long, for example, who took very evident delight in outraging his Senate colleagues. In fact, one of the salient aspects of McCarthy's Senate performances was the utter lack of personal conviction with which they were staged. No matter how outrageous his words, they were nearly always uttered in a deadly monotone; after the most savage personal attacks on colleagues, Joe McCarthy would seek them out for a friendly chat and would evidence genuine dismay to find them offended. Astute capital observers reached the conclusion that McCarthy's "cool" was the "cool" of a complete cynic. He was not in fact deeply dedicated to any of the causes he took up; he simply used them to advance his fortunes or those of his political backers. And unlike other demagogues he did not even bother to disguise his basic indifference—which may have been an indication of the depth of the contempt he felt for his followers. All of these observations suggest basic questions about the personality of the man, his psychological framework, his deepest motivations. These questions will be dealt with in a subsequent chapter; in the meantime we will be content to let the reader make his own inference from the public evidence. By 1950 the Washington press corps had reached at least one conclusion about Joseph R. McCarthy; by unanimous vote they elected him the "worst senator" on Capitol Hill. Not that this dismayed Joe McCarthy: as he himself would have been the first to point out, any publicity is good publicity.

CHAPTER FOUR

The Menace Finds Its Spokesman

> I have here in my hand a list of 205 who were known to
> the secretary of state as being members of the Communist
> Party and who, nevertheless, are still working and
> shaping policy in the State Department.
>
> —SEN. JOSEPH R. MCCARTHY (R., WIS.)

WHILE the distinguished senator from Wisconsin was spending his
first three years in Washington fishing for publicity in the
backwaters of corruption and scandal, that rushing torrent of
humanity's common toils and shocks which we call history had not,
of course, ceased to flow. But Joe McCarthy seemed content to
watch the waves of crisis sweep past with barely a shrug. It is highly
unlikely that he even suspected, as 1949 drew to its close, that he
would soon be swept from his stagnant pools into the deep
mainstream. But in order to understand how this came about, we
must once again examine some of the currents that were soon to
raise the McCarthy tidal wave of hysteria.

It will be recalled that the Democratic Party, smarting from the
defeat it suffered in the 1946 congressional elections, had ascribed
that defeat to Republican accusations of treason, of "being soft on
communism." In a panicky attempt to overcome such charges, the
Democrats were determined to outdo their opponents in combating
the "Menace." Thus, on March 12, 1947, President Harry S
Truman issued Executive Order 9835 which created a loyalty-secu-
rity program for the federal government. By its terms every

government employee (and any employee of private corporations engaged on certain government contracts), be his position ever so humble, would be investigated by the Federal Bureau of Investigation and certain other federal police agencies to determine his loyalty to the United States. If he was found to be "disloyal," he would be considered a security risk and would be fired from his job forthwith. Although loyalty was not the only criterion of what constituted a security risk (alcoholism, dope addiction, sexual "perversion" and just plain talkativeness were other criteria), it was the one that mattered most in the public's imagination.

But to determine whether or not an individual is "loyal" to his nation is a very difficult matter. So varied are the visions of what the United States is, or ought to be, that Americans ranging the political spectrum from anarchists to Fascists have felt themselves more basically loyal to American ideals than were their fellow citizens. Nor would secret spies, saboteurs or disaffected "dupes" be likely to confess themselves enemies of the republic. The determination of loyalty involves investigation of an individual's inner beliefs, thoughts and emotions—a task so difficult and so dangerous to free institutions that it is expressly forbidden by various articles of the Constitution. By the terms of that document, and the English Common Law upon which it was based, a man's opinions, thoughts and beliefs are nobody's business but his own; he is free to hold them and free to advocate them publicly (provided such advocacy does not constitute a "clear and present danger" to public order). On the other hand, the federal government is free to set its own standards of employment, provided those standards meet constitutional requirements. Furthermore, the federal government is not only able but duty-bound to protect itself against enemies, provided the means adopted for such self-protection do not infringe on the constitutional rights of citizens. Yet in times of deep crisis or war (the Civil War being a prime example) the courts have generally allowed the government very wide, even unconstitutional, means to maintain its security. In considering some of the outrageous results of Executive Order 9835 and the apparent indifference with which the American people greeted these results, it is important to remember that the nation felt itself in a time of deep crisis; it was engaged in a new conflict: the Cold War against the Soviet Union and its allies.

By the terms of President Truman's order, the attorney general was to draw up lists of organizations he deemed "subversive" of American ideals or interests. It was left to his personal wisdom to define these difficult terms for his own ends; he was not required to justify his decisions publicly or legally. As a result, the attorney general's office compiled a long list of organizations—some of which had ceased to function decades earlier—which were now labeled "subversive." The list included, for example, certain "committees" established in 1936 to funnel aid and relief to the Spanish Republic during its battle against fascism. It also included various "congresses" set up during the war years as expressions of solidarity between Americans and their then "gallant ally," the Soviet Union. While there was no doubt that many of these organizations had been Communist Party "fronts," secretly controlled by the Party, there was also no doubt that most of their members had been unaware of this and had joined them not because they admired communism but because they agreed with the announced aims of a particular organization. After all, it was not held a crime to be anti-Fascist during the 1930s, or to express friendship for the Soviet Union during World War II; in fact these were more or less national policies. But any and all such organizations that were even suspected of having been tainted by the presence of Communists suddenly became, in the hindsight of 1947, "subversive." And the president's order specifically provided as a standard for dismissal from government employ "Membership in, association with, or sympathetic affiliation with any . . . organization, movement, group or combination of persons, designated by the Attorney General as . . . subversive." Thus actual membership in a real organization was not even the criterion of disloyalty; simple "sympathetic affiliation" with a "combination of persons" would be evidence enough. In other words, if you had contributed a dime to Spanish Relief, had attended a cocktail party at which someone from the Congress of Soviet-American Friendship happened to be present, had been seen talking to someone suspected of belonging to one of the dozens of "subversive" organizations, or had been

59

overheard to make a remark intimating your sympathy for the aims of such an organization, you were suspect. This was the doctrine of "guilt by association" with a vengeance.

Executive Order 9835 also established loyalty review boards for each government department. To these boards the FBI would submit all the pertinent information it had been able to gather about an individual. This information consisted of statements made by an individual's family, friends and associates. FBI agents would dig deep into the past, questioning the suspect's doctors, dentists, landlords, employers—anyone and everyone who could be reached. They would also examine scholastic records, army records, and the records of social and fraternal organizations, as well as those political groups defined as "subversive," to see if they gave any inkling of an individual's political beliefs. In certain cases FBI agents would trail suspects, tap their telephones and secretly examine their mail to determine the present state of their opinions. All of this information, no matter what its value or whence its source, was turned over undigested to the loyalty boards. The testimony of personal enemies eager to say anything to damage a suspect, of estranged wives or husbands who hated their former spouses, of deranged persons whose words were expressions of fantasy—all of this was solemnly taken at face value by the boards.

An individual called on to appear before a loyalty board found himself in a strange world, a world in which English Common Law had never been developed, in which the U.S. Constitution had never been written, in which the Star Chamber and the Spanish Inquisition had triumphed. The suspect was presumed guilty until he could prove his innocence. He was not permitted to know who his accusers were or to face them or to question them even indirectly. He was not even permitted to know what the specific charges were against him! He was simply to know that he was considered disloyal unless he could prove his loyalty. But how does one prove his loyalty? Most of the victims of the loyalty boards pathetically went around gathering testimonials as to their purity from friends or associates. They would produce medals won in their nation's military service. They would make humble statements of their devotion to those aspects of the American Way of Life (capitalism, mom's apple pie, the flag, the Statue of Liberty, etc.)

they hoped would find favor with their persecutors. But in the end they would never know by what criteria they had been adjudged innocent or guilty. If found guilty they did have one recourse—they could appeal to the Loyalty Review Board established to review cases which had been heard by the lower boards. But the procedures of the loyalty review board were exactly the same as those of the subordinate boards. Beyond that, for the wealthy and determined, there was always the possibility of appeal to the courts—a matter which would require years of litigation and thousands of dollars in lawyer's fees.

The penalty for having been found guilty by a loyalty board (and remember that *suspicion* of disloyalty was enough to constitute guilt) was not simply instant dismissal from government service, with the attendant loss of pay and ruined career. Such a dismissal meant that the victim would find it all but impossible to gain employment in private corporations, sensitive as these were about hiring "traitors." The victim's friends often became estranged from him either through disgust or through fear of associating with someone publicly branded as "un-American." It virtually always meant expulsion from the social or professional clubs or organizations of which he had been a member. It often meant that his wife and children were subjected to social or physical abuse. Enforced unemployment and social ostracism resulted in more than a few shattered marriages. In at least two cases the victims, unable to face the ruin of their lives, put an end to them.

Nor was the immediate effect of Executive Order 9835 limited to federal employees. Eager to prove themselves as patriotically alert as the federal government, many states set up loyalty review procedures. These generally bore most heavily upon schoolteachers, university professors, public librarians and others thought to be engaged in "sensitive" (that is to say, intellectual) activities. And various industries hastened to establish loyalty investigations, often using them as a means of dislodging troublesome union leaders. Like a rock tossed into a pond, Executive Order 9835 produced imitative ripples of suspicion and fear over much of the surface of American society.

How did this program of accusation, investigation and judgment increase the security of the United States? Eventually, more than two and one-half million federal employees were to be sifted through the fine screens of the loyalty boards. Of this vast number, by December 1949 exactly 201 individuals had been dismissed as "security risks"—under standards by which even the suspicion of disloyalty became grounds for dismissal. No single case of sabotage or espionage was every uncovered by any of the loyalty boards.

Why, it may be asked, were Americans so supersensitive to that word "loyalty"? Acts of treason have been committed by Americans, just as they have been by Frenchmen, Englishmen, Russians, Chinese, and the nationals of almost every country on the face of the globe. The English have never thought of setting up procedures to root out "un-British Activities," for example. The very concept of "un-French attitudes" would provoke hilarity in France. In the older nations of Europe, as in South America and Asia, the fact of birth is held to confer nationality. No matter how distasteful a man's opinions (and in many countries he can be jailed or executed for them), they are not thought to diminish his nationality. A traitor in England is not considered to be "un-English"—he is an English traitor. A Communist in Italy is not accused by his fellow citizens of being "un-Italian"; he is simply understood by them to be an Italian Communist. Only in the United States has nationality itself been tested by the nature of an individual's beliefs, attitudes or opinions. Yet this is not unnatural. From the very inception of the republic, the quality or attribute of being an "American" has depended more on adherence to a set of political or social doctrines than it has on birth. It was the growth and formulation of those doctrines which originally made "Americans" out of British subjects at the end of the eighteenth century; it was adherence to those doctrines which was required of untold millions of immigrants of very diverse origins seeking to become "Americans" for more than a century thereafter. Thus the very root and nature of the American experience has made the nation hypersensitive to the social and political ideas of its citizens.

Of course, among the ideals and doctrines on which the United States was founded, there were (and still are) other attitudes toward dissent, even dissent that includes the advocacy of overthrowing the United States government, than those assumed in Executive Order 9835. Thomas Jefferson wrote: ". . . If there be any among us who would wish to dissolve this union or to change its republican form, let them stand undisturbed as monuments of the safety with which error of opinion may be tolerated where reason is left free to combat it. . . ." But President Truman was not, alas, Thomas Jefferson; the Democratic Party of 1947 had long ceased to be Jeffersonian (despite the annual lip-service paid by Democrats to their Party's great founder); and evidently the majority of mid-twentieth-century Americans lacked the courage of Jefferson's generation. They were, in fact, very frightened. As we have seen, they had inherited a legacy of fear; Truman's loyalty program, far from assuaging that fear, only institutionalized it.

And a malign fate conspired to fuel American fears at the close of the 1940s with some startling revelations and stunning shocks. Perhaps the key event of that era in the ripening of national hysteria (the seeds of which had been planted long before) was the case of Alger Hiss.

This celebrated affair, which for a while threatened to become a sort of American Dreyfus scandal, originated during the political struggle preceding the presidential election of 1948. The Republicans, still in control of the Eightieth Congress, were seeking any kind of political ammunition to use against the Democrats and their candidate, President Harry S Truman. One of their principal arsenals for the manufacture of such ammunition was the House Committee on Un-American Activities. Summoned to testify before this committee were ex-Communists (some sincere, some professional, some deranged), radical-right paranoids, paid informers —anyone and everyone who was willing to accuse past Democratic administrations of harboring traitors or being "soft on communism." Among those who testified before the committee in August 1948 was self-confessed ex-Communist Whittaker Chambers, then a senior editor on *Time* magazine. Chambers accused nine former government employees of having been secret members of the Communist Party.

The most notable of those accused was Alger Hiss. Hiss had entered government service in the early 1930s. He rose to become director of special political affairs in the State Department, served as an adviser to President Franklin D. Roosevelt at the Yalta conference, and at the Dumbarton Oaks conference helped to draft the Charter of the United Nations. He had retired from the State Department some time before to become head of the Carnegie Endowment for International Peace. He counted as friends Supreme Court justices, presidents of great foundations, many top government officials, and a host of citizens with impeccable credentials.

For dedicated foes of the Menace, as well as Republicans seeking political ammunition, Alger Hiss represented a windfall. If Chambers's accusations were true, then here was proof positive of subversion and treason in the very highest levels of government. Unfortunately, Whittaker Chambers seemed unable to stick to one coherent story. He committed (as was later revealed) perjury in his testimony, though for this he was never prosecuted. Alger Hiss appeared personally before the House Un-American Activities Committee on August 5, 1948, and declared he had never been a Communist or even been affiliated with any Communist organization. A few days later he challenged Whittaker Chambers to repeat his accusations outside the privileged committee hearing room so that he could be sued for libel. On August 27 Chambers repeated his charges on a radio broadcast, and Hiss instituted suit. The entire affair, said President Truman, was a political red herring being dragged across the national consciousness by Republicans eager to detract attention from the miserable record of "that Eightieth do-nothing Congress." Mr. Truman was correct in his own charge, and the Hiss case provided but scanty ammunition to the Republicans before election day, 1948. On that day, scoring one of the most stunning political upsets in American history, President Harry S Truman won reelection and the Democrats regained control of both houses of Congress. It may even be argued that one of the reasons for Truman's surprising victory was public revulsion at Republican tactics.

But the case of Alger Hiss did not end with the presidential election. Early in November 1948, at a pretrial hearing, Whittaker Chambers produced sixty secret State Department documents which, he charged, had been given to him by Alger Hiss during the 1930s. Later, Chambers led House Un-American Activities Committee investigators to his own farm in Maryland, where he produced rolls of microfilm of additional documents secreted in a hollowed-out pumpkin. If Chambers was to be believed, it now appeared that he and Hiss had been not merely Communists, but also leagued spies. Yet because the statute of limitations prohibits prosecution for certain crimes after a lapse of seven years, neither man could be prosecuted for acts of espionage committed thirteen years earlier. Therefore the charge would have to be perjury. After listening to testimony, a grand jury decided on December 15, 1948, that it was probably Hiss who had lied and indicted him for perjury.

The Hiss case now proceeded slowly through the courts, accompanied by all the publicity that the sensation-hungry mass media could derive from it. Appearing as character witnesses for Alger Hiss (either personally or through depositions) were Supreme Court justices, respected educators and high government officials. When questioned by reporters, Secretary of State Dean Acheson declared that "I will never turn my back on Alger Hiss." Thus, to those naturally disposed to political paranoia, the spectacle was presented of a conspiracy on the part of the "establishment" (those hatefully well educated, prissily well dressed, suspiciously well cultivated, immorally sophisticated hedonists on the banks of the Potomac, the Hudson and the Charles rivers) to close ranks to protect one of their own. To the terror inspired in many Americans by the Menace was added the resentment felt by them toward "those striped-pants boys in the State Department" and the "fancy-pants eastern intellectuals." (Why, in the United States, should detestation be universally expressed through a description of a man's pants rather than any other part of his wardrobe?) When the jury at Alger Hiss's first trial declared that it could not reach a decision, the political pressure behind his prosecution was so great that a new trial was immediately ordered; the show would go on.

While American apprehension at the Menace was kept alive by the second Hiss trial, by further investigations by the House Un-American Activities Committee, and by the political uses to which all this was put by both Democratic and Republican politicians, events in the outer world were providing new shocks for the public consciousness.

Perhaps the greatest of these was the victory of Mao Tse-tung's Communist forces in China. The long civil war (it had lasted some

twenty years) between Mao's followers and the Nationalist government of Chiang Kai-shek ended in 1949 with a swift succession of
Communist victories. By the early spring of 1950, Chiang Kai-shek
and his ravaged armies had been driven from the Chinese mainland
to the island of Formosa, where they licked their wounds under the
protecting guns of an American fleet. To many Americans, laboring
under a mistaken notion of the limits of American power, these
events were all but incomprehensible. Had not Chiang Kai-shek
been one of our great allies during World War II? Had not his
armies been trained by American officers and well equipped with
American supplies? Had not the United States sent its most
distinguished soldier-statesman, former Chief of Staff George Catlett Marshall, to China to "sort things out"? To those who held such
thoughts, it was useless to point out that Chiang Kai-shek's
government had grown so corrupt and dictatorial that it could no
longer command the loyalty of the overwhelming majority of the
Chinese people. It was equally useless to point out that, whatever
the rights or wrongs of the matter, the United States, without
committing itself to a full-scale war, simply could not impose its will
on 450 million people with a totally alien social, historical, political
and cultural background ten thousand miles from American shores.
To those whose natural political paranoia was already aroused, the
only explanations for the "loss" of China to the Communists were
perfidy, incompetence and treason within the American government.

The State Department White Paper "explaining" American-
Chinese relations during the postwar years was issued in August
1949. Barely a month later, on September 23, 1949, President
Truman announced that Russia had exploded an atomic "device."
Thus our greatest military secret was secret no longer, and the
Russians could destroy us just as easily as we could destroy them.
To the politically paranoid or naive this was almost as deep a shock
as the "loss" of China. How could the Soviet Union, a nation of
peasants ruled by inept Communist commissars, have developed so
sophisticated a scientific device as an atomic bomb? To those who
cherished an older view of Communist Russia, it was futile to
explain that there was no real "secret" involved in atomic energy,
that knowledge of it was worldwide. It was useless to point out that

the Soviet Union was, in fact, a highly industrialized state with some of the world's finest scientific minds. To many Americans the fact that Russia had develped an atomic bomb only four years after Hiroshima could be explained only by assuming treason and espionage within the American government.

On October 14, 1949, eleven leaders of the American Communist Party, after a trial that in length and notoriety had been almost unprecedented in American history, were found guilty of "conspiring to teach the necessity of overthrowing the American government by force and violence." To those Americans who lived in daily fear of the Menace it was useless to point out that the American Communist Party was one of the most inefficient and stupidly led political organizations in the world; that its membership was minuscule, its influence nil, its political strategy wonderfully self-defeating. Here, with the conviction of its leaders, was proof that the Menace was real and frighteningly sinister.

Then, to cap and climax this "year of shocks" (as some historians have called it), on January 21, 1950, based on evidence the authenticity of which is still questioned by serious critics, the jury in the second Alger Hiss trial brought in a verdict of guilty. This was all that many Americans needed to convince them that their worst suspicions were true. The United States government, under the Roosevelt and now the Truman administrations, obviously had been "soft on communism," had been infested with traitors and spies.

As a matter of fact, there were a few spies in the United States both during and after the Second World War, just as there were spies operating in all the world's leading nations. They were uncovered, however, not by the House Un-American Activities Committee but by the FBI working in cooperation with the British Secret Service. Just two weeks after the conviction of Alger Hiss, the English arrested physicist Klaus Fuchs (who at one time had worked at the American atomic laboratory in Los Alamos, New Mexico) on charges of espionage on behalf of the Soviet Union. His arrest later led to the capture in the United States of Harry Gold, David Greenglass, Morton Sobel and Julius and Ethel Rosenberg, all of whom were later convicted of conspiracy to commit espionage (a crime for which the Rosenbergs were executed). But several very important points should be borne in mind regarding the activities of these spies. First of all, as has already been observed, spying was (and is) a game in which all the leading nations took part; there were (and are) American spies in Russia just as there were (and are) Russian spies in the United States. As long as international relations are carried out on the level of street-gang competition, the adolescent game of spy and counterspy will continue. Secondly, in the opinion of American experts, the information transmitted by the Fuchs ring was so slight and on such a primitive level that it must have been all but valueless to the Soviet Union. Thirdly, while the Rosenbergs, *et al.*, were employed in government-managed laboratories and installations, they were not members of the United States government, nor were they ever employed by it in any policy-shaping or policy-executing position. And, finally, none of these spies were members of the Communist Party. In sum, the capture and conviction of the Fuchs ring of atomic spies no more proved the existence of a widespread political conspiracy to overthrow the United States government than the capture of American spies in Russia proved the existence of a revolutionary American plot to destroy the Soviet regime.

But in the overheated atmosphere of 1949–50, the entire chain of objective international disasters (China's choice for communism, the Soviet development of atomic weapons, etc.), combined with the impact of domestic events such as the trials and conviction of Alger Hiss and the capture of the atomic spies, added fuel to the growing public hysteria about the Menace. And politicians to take advantage of this rising hysteria were not lacking.

It must be repeated that Democrats made use of the Menace just as did Republicans. If Republican campaigners during 1948 and afterward helped whip up national political paranoia to gain office, Democrats already in office committed the same sin to further particular political ends. Thus Democratic Senator Lyndon Baines Johnson used the Menace to prevent the reappointment of Leland Olds to the Federal Power Commission, at the behest of various of his Texas millionaire cronies who were interested in their own private exploitation of natural gas resources. Democratic Senator Pat McCarran of Nevada used an investigation of communism among nationality groups as a means of pushing through his notoriously unfair and xenophobic immigration restriction laws.

Yet, although the Menace was found useful by many politicians of both parties, none had succeeded in making the issue of "communism-in-government" his very own; none had staked his entire career on the anti-Communist hysteria. This was probably due to two factors. First, more than a few politicians undoubtedly entertained scruples about going too far with demagoguery; second, most lacked the imagination and ruthlessness to succeed at it. But there was at least one politician in Washington who combined ruthlessness and imagination with an utter lack of scruples: Senator Joseph R. McCarthy. Ironically, McCarthy's adoption of the cause which was to make him world-famous was almost accidental. It came about in this way.

As the year 1950 opened, the junior senator from Wisconsin had begun to take thought of his approaching reelection campaign. He would have to stand again for the Senate in 1952. But Wisconsin had gone Democratic in the 1948 presidential elections (as it had in the last four out of five), and there were signs that the state's Democrats were preparing to go all out against McCarthy in 1952. Furthermore, some of the senator's shadier financial transactions had become public knowledge in his home state and might provide effective ammunition against him. And finally, McCarthy's record in Washington (the Pepsi-Cola Kid, Water-Boy for the Real Estate Lobby, Defender of the Nazi Malmedy Murderers, the "worst senator") was not one on which he wished to stand for reelection. In the months ahead, Joe McCarthy saw that he would have to make political grist of some popular issue—or face probable defeat in 1952. It was in search of such an issue that McCarthy aide Charles Kraus arranged a dinner for the senator at Washington's Colony Restaurant on January 7, 1950. Present at the table besides McCarthy were Kraus, Washington attorney William A. Roberts, and Father Edmund Walsh, vice-president of Georgetown University. While digesting their meal, the four men racked their brains to find a political issue on which McCarthy could pin his future. Attorney Roberts suggested that he might campaign for the Saint Lawrence seaway project. But McCarthy shook his head. "That hasn't enough appeal," he said. "No one gets excited about it."

Then McCarthy himself suggested that he might campaign on behalf of government pensions of one hundred dollars per month to everyone over the age of sixty-five. But his dinner companions quickly pointed out that such a plan was economically unsound—and besides, with the Social Security system already established, the issue of pensions for the aged was politically dead.

Several other ideas were presented, and then Father Walsh spoke up about a matter that sincerely perturbed him: the menace of communism. Here was not only a vital and popular issue but a very durable one; no doubt the American people would be as interested in the Menace in 1952 as they already were in 1950.

McCarthy seized on this suggestion. "The government is full of Communists," he said in dawning comprehension. "The thing to do is hammer at them!"

Attorney Roberts, a liberal, took alarm. There was already more than enough anti-Communist hysteria abroad in the land, he pointed out; any campaign based on that issue ought to deal in hard facts, not wild accusations. But McCarthy was no longer listening. His eyes were already fixed on the political potential. He'd get the facts easily enough, he muttered. It was plain to Joe's dinner companions that their host was already enthralled by the idea.

In fairness to Kraus, Roberts and Father Walsh, it should be added here that they had no intention of fostering demagoguery. As has been indicated, Roberts was a liberal; Kraus and Father Walsh were sincere anti-Communists who had no inkling of the savage uses McCarthy would make of their faith. All three of these men were soon to denounce Joe McCarthy and his methods.

In a short while the senator had an opportunity to test out his new issue. The traditional Republican Lincoln Day rallies were soon to be held throughout the country, and in preparation for them the Republican National Committee had issued a statement of principles as a guide for Republican orators speaking at Lincoln's Birthday meetings. This statement of principles indicated that the Democrats were to be attacked for "the dangerous degree to which Communists and their fellow-travelers have been employed in important government posts." McCarthy was ready to follow the national committee's guide. Unfortunately, because he was little known in the country at large and because his reputation was none too savory, Senator Joseph McCarthy was not assigned one of the major speaking engagements. He would have to practice his talents before a dinner of about 250 guests sponsored by the Ohio County Women's Republican Club in the small city of Wheeling, West Virginia. Faithful to party directives, McCarthy arrived in Wheeling on February 9, 1950, a rough draft of his intended speech in his hand.

Later there was to be much debate as to exactly what McCarthy said to the Republican ladies of Wheeling and (through radio station WWVA) to the inhabitants of West Virginia. The most reliable report came from Frank Desmond, a reporter for the Wheeling *Intelligencer* who not only heard the speech in person but had a copy of McCarthy's rough draft in his pocket.

McCarthy was in fine form that evening of February 9. His voice quivered with sincerity as he told the ladies that "the fate of the world rests with the clash between the atheism of Moscow and the Christian spirit throughout other parts of the world (*sic*)." Becoming more spirited, McCarthy turned to the case of Alger Hiss. "As you heard this story of high treason," he cried, "I know that you were saying to yourselves, 'Well, why doesn't Congress do something about it?'" Perhaps, McCarthy insinuated, Congress simply reflected a lack of moral vigor on the part of the American people. But in any event there was at least one senator prepared to do his duty. Waving aloft a piece of paper, Joe McCarthy shouted the words with which this chapter opens—words which were to become so notorious that they deserve repetition here:

"I have here in my hand a list of 205 who were known to the secretary of state as being members of the Communist Party and who, nevertheless, are still working and shaping policy in the State Department."

While his audience did not seem particularly startled by this revelation, they gave Senator McCarthy a rousing ovation as he concluded his speech. The senator had little time to enjoy congratulations, however; he had to rush off to his next speaking engagement in Salt Lake City, Utah. There he declared that what he had really said in Wheeling was that there were 205 "bad risks" (which might include others besides Communists) still working in the State Department. In addition, he said, there were 57 "card-carrying Communists" employed in the Department.

McCarthy's next stop was Reno, Nevada. There reporters were handed copies of his Wheeling speech in which the number 205 had been scratched out and the number 57 inserted in its place.

By now (February 11) McCarthy's charges had become front-page copy for more than a few newspapers. After all, if they were true, they made a sensational story. The State Department itself had already reacted by sending McCarthy a telegram demanding the names of the 205 suspects, who, they assured him, would be swiftly investigated. McCarthy had not replied to this telegram. Instead, on a radio broadcast from Salt Lake City, he had declared: "Now, I want to tell the secretary [of state] this: If he wants to call me tonight at the Utah Hotel, I will be glad to give him the names of those 57 card-carrying Communists. . . ."

From Reno, Nevada, McCarthy fired off a telegram to the president of the United States stating that "I have in my possession the names of 57 Communists who are in the State Department at present." He did not offer to submit these names, however. Instead he informed President Truman that he could secure them from the files of the State Department's loyalty board. Evidently Senator McCarthy did not consider the activities of these alleged 57 Communists dangerous enough to warrant submission of the list to the FBI instantly. On the other hand, his tactics were arousing a storm of publicity—and this was what was most important to him.

Perhaps emboldened by all the publicity, McCarthy in Reno named for the first time some specific individuals who he implied were security risks employed in the State Department. These individuals were John W. Service, Mrs. Mary Jane Keeney, Gustavo Duran and Dr. Harlow Shapley.

Though it was true that there was a John S. Service employed in the State Department (not John W.) as a Far Eastern specialist, Gustavo Duran had not been in the department's employ since 1946; Mrs. Mary Jane Keeney (who had worked for the State Department for four months) had resigned also in 1946; and Dr. Harlow Shapley, a distinguished astronomer, had never been employed by the State Department.

Reckless as these accusations were, they were no less reliable than were Joe McCarthy's very specific numbers—either the number 205 or the number 57—of supposed "card-carrying Communists" undermining the nation's security from their desks in the State Department. These numbers came from two sources. The number 205 was derived from a letter written in July 1946 by Secretary of State James F. Byrnes in which he referred to 205 State Department employees then undergoing investigation by loyalty boards. The number 57 came from the files of the House Appropriations Committee of the Eightieth Congress, which in 1947 had compiled a list of 57 *possible* suspects employed by the State Department. That these were lists of people undergoing investigation, not conviction; that the lists were three or four years old; that they included not only State Department employees but also people who were simply *applying* for jobs in the department—none of this mattered to Joe McCarthy. As he now realized, he had found the issue he'd been seeking. Wherever he went now he was surrounded by reporters; his name and photograph decorated the pages of the nation's press. From obscurity tinged with scandal he had hoisted himself into the limelight as a crusader against the Menace.

Since both the number 205 and the number 57 (as well as an abacus full of other numbers used by the senator) were soon to be discredited, many people have long wondered just what that "list of 205" was that McCarthy waved aloft in Wheeling, West Virginia. Although it cannot now be proved, an anecdote related by Fred J. Cook in his book *The Nightmare Decade* has the ring of truth:

"A personal friend of mine," writes Cook, "a journalist who was once a close friend of McCarthy's, asked him on one occasion: 'Joe, just what did you have in your hand down there in Wheeling?'

"McCarthy gave his characteristic roguish grin and replied, 'An old laundry list.' "

CHAPTER FIVE

The Senator Attacks

Someone whose identity is not yet officially determined is lying at the rate Ananias never lied.

—Sen. Mathew Neeley (d., w.va.)

McCARTHY'S OFF RECORD RANTINGS PURE MOONSHINE STOP DELIGHTED HIS WHOLE CASE RESTS ON ME AS THIS MEANS HE WILL FALL FLAT ON HIS FACE STOP

—Owen Lattimore

On the evening of February 20, 1950, Senator Joseph R. McCarthy, fresh from his sensational appearances in Wheeling, Salt Lake City and Reno, entertained the United States Senate with one of the most remarkable performances that august body had ever witnessed. His briefcase bulging with photostatic copies of State Department loyalty board case-history files, the junior senator from Wisconsin undertook to substantiate his charges of "disloyalty" and "Communist infiltration" in the executive branch of the government. He had, he claimed, the documentary evidence of widespread treason and espionage—evidence embodied in 108 case histories (yes, the number had changed again), 81 of which he undertook to read on the Senate floor. As it later developed, the Senator's arithmetic was not quite accurate; he omitted some of the 81 cases and repeated others in his long and rambling dissertation.

How had Joe McCarthy come into possession of this "fresh" and "startling" information? The files of the government's loyalty boards had been closed to Congress by Executive Order of President

Truman in 1948—an order the president had issued precisely to protect the reputations of possibly innocent individuals against public smearing. But, McCarthy informed his colleagues, he had had the help of "some good, loyal Americans in the State Department." He would not reveal who these patriotic spies were, because "I know the State Department is very eager to know how I have secured all this information. I know that the jobs of the men who helped me secure this material would be worth nothing if the names were given." Senator McCarthy declared modestly that he had "pierced the Truman iron curtain of secrecy" surrounding the activities of "traitors" in the government.

All of which was a lie. What McCarthy actually had were copies of some one hundred individual dossiers prepared in 1947 from the State Department loyalty files by investigators from the House Appropriations Committee. This collection of case histories (they were actually summaries of loyalty board findings) was neither new nor particularly startling; several copies of the collection were in circulation among senators and in the files of various Senate and House committees. Furthermore, this ancient material was so inaccurate, so hopelessly prejudiced and so unsubstantiated that even the eager researchers of the Republican-controlled Eightieth Congress had been unable to extract political ammunition from it.

None of this, of course, troubled Senator McCarthy; he was prepared to rush in where even House Un-American Activities Committee investigators feared to tread. Nor, during his reading of these case histories, did his imagination fail him. For example, case number 40 from the House files read:

"This employee is with the Office of Information and Educational Exchange in New York City.

"His application is very sketchy. There has been no investigation. (C-8) is a reference. Though he is 43 years of age, his file reflects no history prior to June 1941."

McCarthy read this to the Senate as his case number 36:

"This individual is 43 years of age. He is with the Office of Information and Education. According to the file, he is a known Communist. I might say that when I refer to someone as being a known Communist, I am not evaluating the information myself. I am merely giving what is in the file. This individual also found his

75

way into the Voice of America broadcast. Apparently the easiest way to get in is to be a Communist."

And so it went, case after case distorted beyond recognition or invented on the spot, for hour after hour. How did Senator McCarthy's colleagues react to this interminable diatribe? First of all, many of them tried to avoid it altogether. When McCarthy rose to speak there were barely fifteen senators present. But at the instigation of Senator Kenneth Wherry, a Nebraska Republican who was Senate minority leader (and an ardent fan of McCarthy), the Senate's sergeant-at-arms was dispatched to round up reluctant senators and compel them to attend the performance—the first time in five years that such an extraordinary step had been taken.

Several of the Democratic senators present attempted to pin McCarthy down on his own very obvious distortions. Majority leader Senator Scott Lucas (D., Ill.) rose to ask whether McCarthy was aware that the loyalty boards (the efficiency and patriotism of which McCarthy was attacking) had been staffed, by President Truman's order, by rock-ribbed Republicans and that the entire loyalty review structure was headed by arch-Republican Seth Richardson? McCarthy seemed stunned by this information—but only momentarily. With superb effrontery he opined that, obviously, loyalty boards would be the first target for Communist infiltration.

Senator Brien McMahon (D., Conn.) rose to ask McCarthy whether he had the complete files of the cases he was reciting. McCarthy admitted he did not.

"Does not the senator realize," McMahon demanded, "that if I were to send investigators into his state, perhaps I could obtain 105 or perhaps 1,005 witnesses who would make statements about the senator that would be totally untrue and incorrect. . . . Did the senator ever think of that?"

McCarthy responded that he believed he was giving a "fair" version of what the files contained.

McMahon would not be appeased. "I call attention to the possibility that, if we had the whole file before us, as undoubtedly the State Department has, the information the senator from Wisconsin is giving the Senate might be contradicted . . .," he said.

This was too dangerously close to the truth to be accepted by McCarthy's fellow Republicans (at least some of whom must have known he was lying). Senator Karl Mundt (R., S.D.) jumped up to declare: "I hope the senator [McCarthy] will not follow the suggestion of the senator from Connecticut and discontinue his efforts to purge Communists from the government."

". . . The senator from Connecticut made no such statement," McMahon protested. "I say to the senator [Mundt]," he shouted, "that what we have to be careful of is that we do not imitate the very thing we are against. Star Chambers are not for the United States of America, nor are trials *ex parte,* on the basis of part of the files of the persons concerned, on the floor of the United States Senate, the way to handle the matter."

But what about Alger Hiss? Mundt countered. Had Congress depended on legal niceties, Hiss never would have been convicted. Other Republican senators present murmured agreement. McMahon found himself deserted by members of his own party and was drowned out in the clamor. McCarthy droned on undisturbed until just before midnight, having treated the Senate to an exhibition of falsification, distortion and arrogance such as it had rarely witnessed.

Both the Democratic and the Republican leaderships in Congress realized that a major political fight was brewing. If Republican senators would willingly support McCarthy in his wild accusations, then to the Democratic strategists that meant that the Republican Party was prepared to make communism in government the central theme of the approaching presidential campaign of 1952. The pressures to conduct a formal and public investigation of McCarthy's charges could no longer be resisted. And since that was the case, the Democratic Senate leadership determined to set up and control the investigation themselves. The Republicans would no doubt try by every means to substantiate at least some of McCarthy's charges; the Democrats would attempt to show that the senator from Wisconsin was a liar. Accordingly, when the Senate convened on the day following McCarthy's speech, the Democrats introduced Senate Resolution 231, which authorized a complete and impartial investigation of McCarthy's charges. After a certain amount of political maneuvering this resolution was adopted.

Authority over the investigation was given to the Senate Foreign Relations Committee (since McCarthy's charges involved State Department personnel). This committee in turn appointed a special subcommittee to handle the matter.

Chairman of the subcommittee was Maryland Democrat Millard Tydings, a suave, conservative, tough politician who could be counted on to "handle" McCarthy without kid gloves. His Democratic colleagues on the subcommittee would be Senators Brien McMahon of Connecticut and Theodore F. Green of Rhode Island. These senators too could be trusted to deflate the McCarthy charges. Two Republicans completed the membership of the subcommittee: Henry Cabot Lodge of Massachusetts and Bourke B. Hickenlooper of Iowa. Lodge was entirely too much the aristocrat to sympathize with McCarthy's techniques and had long been respected as a Republican "liberal." McCarthy's only avowed supporter on the subcommittee was Bourke Hickenlooper, the Iowa senator whose witlessness and fumbling had long since made his name synonymous on Capitol Hill with incompetence.

Even before he knew the names of the men who would investigate his charges in public hearings, Joe McCarthy knew he was in trouble. The extravagance of his statements had turned many powerful fellow Republicans against him. "Mr. Republican" himself, Senator Robert A. Taft, had described McCarthy's Senate speech as "a perfectly reckless performance." The Republican leadership feared that by demolishing McCarthy, the Democrats might also demolish anticommunism as a juicy political issue. As for professional exploiters of the red scare outside Congress, many at first felt that the appearance of such a "clown" as McCarthy in their ranks could only damage their cause.

But if Joe McCarthy faced powerful opposition, he gained powerful support. To his aid came newspaper magnates Colonel Robert R. McCormick and William Randolph Hearst. Not only did newspaper chains and radio stations controlled by these publishing titans assure McCarthy of widespread and sympathetic publicity; through them the services of some of the shrewdest and most famous Menace peddlers in the country were made available. Thus McCormick dispatched such newsmen as Willard Edwards of the *Chicago Tribune* to McCarthy's aid, while Hearst assigned such renowned pundits as George Sokolsky, Westbrook Pegler, Howard Rushmore and Fulton Lewis, Jr., to McCarthy's camp. These columnists and reporters were old hands at fishing in the troubled waters of anticommunism; from past "exposés" and dusty "research" files much additional material was funneled to the senator's office. A particularly valuable aide proved to be J. B. Matthews, a Hearst employee who had made a sort of pilgrim's progress from Methodist preacher to fellow-traveler to disillusioned leftist to professional expert on the Menace. And, to help him weather the approaching storm, McCarthy personally hired a private investigator named Don Surine who had recently been fired from the FBI for improper behavior.

Also at McCarthy's side there now appeared textile importer Arthur Kohlberg, a leading member of what was known in Washington as the "China Lobby." This remarkable group included all those who hoped to reverse the verdict of history in Asia, to secure somehow the triumph of Chiang Kai-shek's Nationalists in China over the Communist government of Mao Tse-tung. Some members of the China Lobby were (like Kohlberg) industrialists who had lost Asiatic markets or sources of supply; some were "old China hands" such as missionaries, diplomats or soldiers who had once been stationed in China but were now, of course, excluded from that nostalgically remembered "good life"; some were high military strategists concerned with the loss of potentially vital American bases in Asia; some were public-relations men hired by the Chiang Kai-shek regime to agitate for continued American support. Many of the members of the China Lobby were expressing views which simply developed from selfish personal interest, but almost all members sincerely believed that China had been "lost" because of the machinations of a powerful Communist conspiracy in the higher echelons of the United States government. McCarthy's charges against the State Department fitted in perfectly with the aims of the China Lobby, and these people hastened to provide the senator with their well-financed assistance.

Despite all this, when the Tydings Committee hearings opened on March 8, 1950, the junior senator from Wisconsin was put on the defensive immediately. Senator Tydings, a powerful and canny politician, opened the proceedings with an instant demand that

Senator Millard Tydings grimly assures McCarthy: "You are going to get one of the most complete investigations in the history of this country." McCarthy, grinning, has evidently missed the full implications of Tydings's remark.

McCarthy provide names, dates and specific references to back up his charges. When McCarthy attempted to evade his questions, the Maryland Democrat simply grew more insistent. He would not even permit McCarthy the usual courtesy of delivering an opening statement; he attacked at once. So heavy was Tydings's determined onslaught that the Republican members of the subcommittee protested. Of course the Tydings tactics were designed to expose the McCarthy charges as fraudulent from the very outset of the hearings. But the tactics backfired. The Tydings onslaught provided both McCarthy and his Republican backers with a perfect propaganda ploy with which to obscure the real issues: McCarthy, a solitary David, was pitted against the Goliath of government bureaucracy, and was being crucified by the Democrats. Why? Obviously to protect the reputation of the Democratic administration and its State Department. In other words, the hearings were really an attempt to "whitewash" the State Department by destroying McCarthy. This public display of martyrdom, which continued for days and weeks (neither Tydings nor Brien McMahon would relent in his caustic and persistent demolishing of McCarthy's charges) suited McCarthy perfectly. It was precisely the picture he hoped to paint of himself before his constituents and the American people. Here again was honest, brave Tail-Gunner Joe, fighting against great odds to defend the republic against insidious enemies—and his efforts were being sabotaged by politicians afraid of exposure. Actually, the tactics employed by Tydings were far kinder and infinitely more straightforward than the tactics McCarthy himself used later when he served as chairman of various investigating committees. And if McCarthy claimed he was being "crucified," that was true; but his crucifixion grew from the fact—apparent to everyone who followed the proceedings—that his dramatic charges of treason, conspiracy and espionage in the State Department were totally untrue. Of the several public accusations he made before the Tydings Committee, three were notable in themselves and as examples of the falsity of all his other accusations.

The first of these involved a distinguished lawyer and former judge from New York City, Dorothy Kenyon. Miss Kenyon, McCarthy informed the committee, had been "affiliated with at least twenty-eight Communist-front organizations." Not only that, the senator said, "The Communist activities of Miss Kenyon . . . extend back through the years. It is inconceivable that this woman could collaborate with a score of organizations dedicated to the overthrow of our form of government by force and violence, participate in their activities, lend her name to their nefarious purposes, and be ignorant of the whole sordid and un-American aspect of their work." Furthermore, McCarthy pointed out, the "case" of Dorothy Kenyon was "extremely important in that it will shed considerable light on the workings of our loyalty program."

These were very grave charges. On what were they based? First of all, it turned out that Miss Kenyon, although she had once held an honorary position on a United Nations committee on women's rights, had never been employed by the State Department in any capacity whatsoever. Therefore, of course she had never gone through the Department's loyalty review processes. So whereas the case might "shed considerable light" on something, it certainly could shed no light on either the supposed Communist infiltration of the State Department or the "workings of our loyalty program."

What, in fact, it did shed light on was the essential recklessness and cowardice of McCarthy's accusations. For Miss Kenyon, a liberal, generous and active woman of high professional and intellectual attainments, treated McCarthy and his charges with the contempt they deserved. She called the Wisconsin senator "an unmitigated liar" and pointed out that "Senator McCarthy comes from Wisconsin, sometimes called the state of the great winds. He is a wonderful example." And on behalf of herself and the American Civil Liberties Union (of which she had been a director since 1931) Miss Kenyon challenged McCarthy to repeat his charges outside the Senate so that he could be sued for slander. "Senator McCarthy is a coward to take shelter in the cloak of congressional immunity," she declared. But this was a challenge to which McCarthy was never to respond.

Dorothy Kenyon appeared before the Tydings Committee on March 14, 1950, and although she had previously invited Joe McCarthy to be present for a personal confrontation, the senator absented himself. In so doing he was very wise, for it quickly developed that the lady judge was equipped with far more honesty and just plain guts than Tail-Gunner Joe.

"I am not and never have been a Communist," Miss Kenyon testified. "I am not and never have been a fellow-traveler. I am not and never have been a supporter of, or member of, or a sympathizer with, any organization known to me to be, or suspected by me of being, controlled or dominated by Communists. . . . If this leaves anything unsaid to indicate my total and complete detestation of that political philosophy, it is impossible for me to express my sentiments. I mean my denial to be all-inclusive."

As for her "affiliation" with "twenty-eight Communist-front organizations," it turned out that many of the organizations listed by McCarthy were not, in fact, listed as either subversive or "Communist-front" on the attorney general's roll of suspect organizations. Where Miss Kenyon admitted affiliation with organizations that *were* so listed, it inevitably turned out that she had aligned herself with them many years before they had come under the attorney general's surveillance, always because they ostensibly were

The junior senator from Wisconsin informs the Tydings subcommittee that the State Department is "riddled" with Communists. Seated from left to right: Senators Henry Cabot Lodge, Jr. (R., Mass.); Bourke Hickenlooper (R., Iowa); Millard Tydings (D., Md.), chairman; Theodore F. Green (D., R.I.); Brien McMahon (D., Conn.) and onlooker Tom Connally (D., Tex.).

devoted to causes in which she was interested (such as aid to the Spanish Republic, or women's rights), and in each case she had resigned from an organization once it became clear that it was, in fact, subservient to Communist influence. If anything, Miss Kenyon was an outspoken anti-Communist (of the liberal, not the paranoid variety), and in her role as a delegate to the United Nations Commission on the Status of Women she had declared: "Women in Russia undoubtedly have more equality in a greater number of jobs than do American women, but it is the equality of slavery," thereby drawing down upon herself the wrath of the Russian delegation and the diatribes of Radio Moscow.

In her final summation Miss Kenyon said:

". . . I am a lover of democracy, of individual freedom, and of human rights for everybody; a battler, perhaps a little too much of a battler sometimes, for the rights of the little fellow who gets forgotten or frightened or shunned because of unpopular views. . . .

Dictatorship, cruelty, oppression and slavery are to me intolerable. I cannot live in their air; I must fight back. This is not perhaps a very wise or prudent way to live, but it is my way."

Even McCarthy backer Bourke Hickenlooper was forced to admit that there was neither "the least evidence" to show nor "the least belief" in his mind that Miss Kenyon had ever been "in any way subversive or disloyal." And that terminated the first specific accusation made by McCarthy to demonstrate "Communist infiltration of the State Department."

The second target of McCarthy's innuendos was one of the most prestigious of American diplomats, Philip C. Jessup, United States ambassador at large. In an aside (one is tempted to say a "stage whisper") during his attack upon Dorothy Kenyon, McCarthy had mentioned Ambassador Jessup as having "an unusual affinity . . . for Communist causes." Then, as his "case" against Miss Kenyon quickly crumbled to bits, McCarthy strengthened his charges against Jessup. The ambassador, he declared, was "now formulating top-flight policy in the Far East affecting half the civilized world." Furthermore, he informed reporters, Jessup had been a sponsor of the American-Russian Institute, an organization later cited as subversive by the attorney general. The mere mention of Philip Jessup's name was sufficient to provoke banner headlines in the nation's press, headlines which helped to obscure the collapse of McCarthy's attack on Dorothy Kenyon. It was also sufficient to bring Ambassador Jessup hurrying home from a fact-finding tour of the Far East that he was undertaking for the State Department. On March 20, 1950, Ambassador Jessup appeared before the Tydings Committee.

Like Judge Kenyon, Philip Jessup was forced to undergo the essential humiliation of reviewing his entire life as if justifying himself before the Gates of Heaven. His family background was impressive: the ancestors who had arrived during the seventeenth century; the great-grandfather who had helped nominate Abraham Lincoln for the presidency in 1860; the father who had been a stout supporter of the Presbyterian church—all impeccably conservative, impeccably Anglo-Saxon. Then the trotting forth of facts from his own life calculated to demonstrate his "Americanism": his service as a private in the infantry during World War I; his first job as an assistant to the president of the First National Bank in Utica, New York; the fact that he had once been superintendent of the Sunday School of the First Presbyterian Church; that his mentor had been Republican elder statesman Elihu Root; that he had served as an ambassador to Cuba for the arch-conservative administration of President Herbert Hoover; that in recent years, as American delegate to the United Nations, he had endured many a shouting match with the Russian representatives (and had generally won); that he had been consistently libeled and attacked by the Soviet press as a dyed-in-the-dollar anti-Communist; even, finally, that he had been a commander of his local American Legion post and was still an active member of that 180 percent American organization of vigilant patriots.

Following this review, Ambassador Jessup produced testimonials as to his patriotism from Generals George C. Marshall and Dwight D. Eisenhower. Marshall wrote: "Throughout your entire service with me while I was Secretary of State you were clearly outstanding as a representative of the Government both as to your masterful presentations and the firmness of your opposition to all Soviet or Communist attacks or pressures." Dwight Eisenhower declared: "Your long and distinguished record . . . has won for you the respect of your colleagues and of the American people as well. No one who has known you can for a moment question the depth of sincerity of your devotion to the principles of Americanism."

But what about the ambassador's sponsorship of the American-Russian Institute? Alas, it turned out that Jessup had never "sponsored" the American-Russian Institute. On two occasions he had permitted that organization (then, be it remembered, *not* under suspicion by the attorney general) to use his name, along with the names of hundreds of other distinguished citizens, as a "sponsor" of two dinners given by the institute—one of which had as its "subversive" intent the paying of tribute to the memory of President Franklin D. Roosevelt shortly after his death.

Feeling the ground shifting beneath his feet, McCarthy now loosed broadsides of accusations seeking to link Ambassador Jessup with Frederick Vanderbilt Field, an avowed Communist who had worked with Jessup as a member of the Institute of Pacific Relations. The institute itself (long a favorite target of right-wing extremists and the propagandists of the China Lobby) was basically an organization devoted to the gathering and dissemination of expert American opinion on Asian affairs. Its purpose was the promotion of better understanding of far eastern problems. It was financed by large American corporations with far eastern interests. Associated with it were such undeniably capitalistic businessmen as Henry R. Luce, publisher of *Life, Time* and *Fortune*; Juan Trippe, president of Pan American Airways; and William Herrod, later president of International General Electric Company. Yet it was certainly true that Jessup had been active on various institute committees at the same time that Frederick Vanderbilt Field (scion of an immensely wealthy midwestern department store family) had been the Institute's financial "angel." Furthermore, on several occasions Jessup had expressed his high regard for Field's abilities. Did Jessup know that Field was a Communist? No; not the faintest shred of evidence could be found that he did. Here again was an attempt to establish "guilt by association" on the coarsest possible level.

Meeting this nebulous charge, Jessup told the committee: "By this theory, the wartime photographs of American GIs shaking hands with Russian troops in Germany would mean that the GIs were guilty of communism by association." He might also have added that every American, of high or low degree, who had ever dealt with any Soviet citizen would likewise be guilty.

Senator Hickenlooper, apparently baffled by this line of reasoning, now brought up the fact that Ambassador Jessup (like so many of his more distinguished colleagues) had appeared as a character witness for Alger Hiss.

"It is my understanding," Jessup retorted, "that there is a very simple part of our American system under which a person accused is entitled to have testimony regarding his reputation."

Despite the degradation of having to answer these charges before such men as Hickenlooper, it turned out that Jessup was much more concerned with the impact of these hearings on the reputation of the United States abroad than he was with his own fate. He was, after all, American ambassador at large, reporting not only to the State Department but also to the president. He was not merely a "fact-finder" but also an intermediary between the United States government and foreign regimes.

"If Senator McCarthy's innuendoes were true," Jessup pointed out, "the representatives of foreign governments with whom I spoke would be entitled to believe that my statements to them were deceitful and fraudulent. They would be entitled to believe that no confidence should be placed in the declarations which I made on behalf of our government. If it were true that the president and the secretary of state had sent on such a mission a person who was a traitor to his own government they might well feel that they could place no confidence in the statements made by any of the representatives of the United States abroad.

"It may be relatively unimportant whether the character of a single American citizen is blackened and his name is brought into disrepute, but in the present serious situation of international relations throughout the world today, it is a question of the utmost gravity when an official holding the rank of ambassador at large of the United States of America is held up before the eyes of the rest of the world as a liar and a traitor. I am aware, Mr. Chairman, that Senator McCarthy has not used those words. But if his insinuations were true, those words would certainly be appropriate."

This appeal to patriotism had no apparent effect on the committee members. All of them knew these words were true; all of them knew that Ambassador Jessup was certainly not a Communist or even a Communist sympathizer. But they had to proceed with the charade through fear of political consequences. That is to say, they felt themselves forced to cater to the paranoid frenzies of the China Lobby, because they feared that their own constituents would rise against them in wrath if they did not. The rapturous reception McCarthy's accusations received at public meetings, the high-intensity press coverage, their own mail from home—all of these cowed committee members. It was never a question of Jessup's guilt (the Tydings Committee completely exonerated the ambassador of all charges within a few days)—it was rather a question of continuing a farcical public demonstration of the most depressing weaknesses in the American body politic. What Ambassador Jessup failed to point out in his statement was the apparent fact that whereas foreign governments were well aware that he was not in fact a traitor to his own country, and that they could therefore continue to place confidence in the loyalty of the president and the secretary of state, the very spectacle of the committee hearings must have inevitably led all impartial observers to question, not the fidelity of the servants of the United States government, but rather the sanity of its legislative branch. In this respect it is instructive to note that little more than a year after Philip Jessup had been "cleared" by the Tydings Committee, the Senate Foreign Relations Committee refused to confirm his nomination as a delegate to the United Nations—entirely on the basis and as a result of McCarthy's disproved allegations.

And even as Jessup was humiliating himself before the Tydings Committee, Senator McCarthy, apprehensive now that his charges so far had been successfully rebutted by each of his intended victims and very much aware that he needed something "big" to divert public attention from this fiasco, began hinting to the press that he was ready to name "the top Russian espionage agent in the United States." For several days McCarthy toyed with eager reporters as to just who this red ogre might be (while headlines about the impending "revelation" thrust the Tydings Committee hearings on Jessup onto the back pages of the nation's press), and at last, on March 21, 1950, he declared that his "top Russian spy" was Professor Owen J. Lattimore, then director of the Walter Hines Page School of International Relations at Johns Hopkins University.

Apprised of this "sensational" leak to the press, Senator Tydings immediately called his committee into (closed) executive session to hear fuller details from McCarthy himself. But instead of presenting any solid evidence to the committee, McCarthy contented himself with declaring that "There is nothing mysterious about this one. This has all been put in the record already, plus some exhibits." He said that Lattimore was "definitely an espionage agent," that the case was "explosive." "If you crack this case," Joe solemnly declared, "it will be the biggest espionage case in the history of the country." When committee members pressed him for facts, Senator McCarthy loftily pointed out that all they had to do was examine the loyalty and security files to find all the proof they needed. Later he told reporters, "I'm willing to stand or fall on this one." To reporters and others who had never heard of Professor Owen Lattimore, Joe McCarthy made one of the most remarkable statements of his remarkable career. Owen Lattimore? "I believe," he gravely declared, "you can ask almost any school child who is the architect of our far eastern policy, and he will say 'Owen Lattimore.' "

The subject of McCarthy's charges and of mounting speculation in the press had never been a regular member of the State Department, although he had held several government posts and was a highly respected authority on far eastern affairs. Owen Lattimore had spent much of his childhood in China, had later been in the export-import business in Shanghai, had explored much of the little-known interior of Central Asia, had lectured to various geographic societies, and had written several fascinating travel books, among them *Desert Road to Turkestan* and *High Tartary*, about his adventures. He had witnessed the Japanese invasion of Manchuria and North China during the 1930s and, like many others in China, had thrown his support to Chiang Kai-shek as the nation's best possible war leader. In 1941 (before America's entrance into World War II) Lattimore had been appointed by Chiang Kai-shek as his "personal American aide." Although this appointment had the blessing of President Franklin D. Roosevelt, Lattimore had no connection with the U.S. government. After Pearl Harbor Professor Lattimore had left Chiang to become deputy director of the Office of War Information in Washington. He had traveled to Chiang's wartime capital, Chungking, in 1942 and later that year accompanied Madame Chiang Kai-shek when she visited San Francisco. In 1944 he had been a member of Vice-President Henry Wallace's fact-finding mission that journeyed to China and Siberia. Although often consulted by the State Department after the war, Lattimore was never employed by it in any official capacity. At the time of McCarthy's attack he was in Kabul, Afghanistan, with a United Nations mission exploring the possibilities of economic aid to that country.

Like almost all American far eastern experts, Owen Lattimore had long since become disillusioned with Chiang Kai-shek. He had seen Chiang's regime in China crumble from its own inner weaknesses: corruption, brutality, militarism, and total indifference to the desperate needs of China's millions. Like many another American "old China hand," while stoutly anti-Communist, Lattimore had clearly foreseen and warned against the eventual triumph of Mao Tse-tung's Communist Party in that war-racked land. Later, in a book entitled *The Situation in Asia* (1949), Lattimore had predicted war in Korea and urged against American involvement in France's losing battle against the independence movement in Vietnam. Needless to say, these prescient views had earned Lattimore the undying hatred of the China Lobby. Almost all the material McCarthy employed against Lattimore was supplied from the vivid imagination of such China Lobby types as Arthur Kohlberg.

A slight, balding individual who looked every inch the scholar, Lattimore rose courageously to defend himself. Apprised by a cable from the Associated Press of McCarthy's charges, he immediately fired off the cable answer reproduced at the beginning of this chapter and prepared to return home from Afghanistan.

Perhaps aware of the fact that he had really put himself out onto a long and shaky limb this time, Joe McCarthy improved the days before Lattimore's return by making a long (four-hour), rambling denunciation of his victim to the United States Senate. On March 30 Joe informed his colleagues that he had a witness who would testify that Lattimore had been "high up" in Communist Party circles for years. Furthermore, he would demonstrate that Secretary of State Dean Acheson was no more than "the voice and mind of Lattimore."

Senator Herbert Lehman demanded: "Have you made available to the [Tydings] subcommittee the information of which you are now speaking?"

"The answer is 'No.' "

"Why is the answer 'No'?"cried Lehman. "That is the place to which charges should be referred rather than to submit here only parts of your charges. . . . You are making a spectacle to the galleries here and to the public where a man accused has no chance to answer!"

McCarthy cried out: "The traitors will cause many men not to have a chance. . . . Crocodile tears are being shed here for

Professor Owen Lattimore (left foreground) leaves a session of the Tydings subcommittee hearings ahead of the man whose charges were to follow the Asia expert for many, many years.

traitorous individuals, but forgotten are 400,000,000 people who have been sold into slavery by these people!"

The galleries applauded wildly.

But on April 1 it was Owen Lattimore's turn. Arriving in Washington, he told a press conference that McCarthy was "a base and miserable creature" who was "telling the kind of lies about the United States that Russian propagandists could not invent." Five days later, testifying before the Tydings Committee, Lattimore accused McCarthy of violating the responsibility of his high office.

"He has violated it," Lattimore declared, "by impairing the effectiveness of the United States government in its relations with its friends and allies, and by making the government of the United States an object of suspicion in the eyes of the anti-Communist world, and undoubtedly the laughing-stock of Communist governments.

"He has violated it by instituting a reign of terror among officials and employees of the United States government, no one of whom can be sure of safety from attack by the machine gun of irresponsible publicity in Joseph McCarthy's hands.

"He has without authorization used secret documents obtained from government files. He has vilified citizens of the United States and accused them of high crime without giving them an opportunity to defend themselves.

"He has refused to submit alleged documentary evidence to a duly constituted committee of the Senate.

"He has invited disrespect to himself and his high office by refusing to live up to his word. Twice on the floor of the Senate he stated that any charges he made under the cloak of immunity, he would repeat in another place so that their falseness could be tested in a court of the United States. He said that if he should fail to do this he would resign. He has been called to repeat his charges so that they could be tested in a court of action. He has failed to do so. And he has not resigned."

The object of this stinging denunciation, the junior senator from Wisconsin, looked everywhere around the crowded committee chamber except at his accuser. He sat pale and impassive, a spectator at the funeral of his own reputation. And if the pugnacity of Lattimore's statement came as a surprise to onlookers (who interrupted it several times with applause), Senator Tydings had an even more shattering surprise up his sleeve. After Lattimore had concluded, the Maryland senator declared: ". . . I owe it to you and to the country to tell you that four members of this subcommittee recently had a complete summary of your loyalty file read to us in the presence of Mr. J. Edgar Hoover, head of the Federal Bureau of Investigation.

"At the conclusion of the reading, it was the unanimous opinion of all members of the subcommittee and of all others in the room (this included United States Attorney General J. Howard McGrath) that there is nothing in the files to show that you have ever been a Communist or have ever been connected with espionage."

It would seem that the first round of the Lattimore-McCarthy battle had gone to the professor. But McCarthy, having stated that he would "stand or fall on this one," was not prepared to give up easily. On April 20 he produced his surprise witness in the form of Louis Budenz, former high Communist Party official and ex-editor of the *Daily Worker*. Mr. Budenz, like many of his Communist brethren, had years before experienced total conversion. He had been so disillusioned by one or another facet of Party policy or doctrine that the entire structure of his Marxist faith had come toppling down—only to be replaced by another, Catholicism. With much the same muddle-headed fanaticism with which he had once embraced the extreme left, he now embraced the extreme right. From 1946 to 1949 Budenz had spent many hours telling the FBI everything he knew, imagined or supposed about the Communist apparatus in the United States. He had become, in effect, a government informer. Oddly enough, during all those years of patient probing and grilling by the FBI, Budenz had never mentioned the name of Owen Lattimore. Now, however, perhaps at the urging of McCarthy's special assistant, Don Surine, Budenz came forward.

His testimony before the Tydings Committee turned out to be somewhat less than sensational. He had "heard" this; he had "thought" that; he had been "reliably informed" by someone whose name he'd forgotten; he had "assumed" something else—in short, he was able to produce not one single specific instance that would remotely link Owen Lattimore with the Communist Party or the Communist underground in America. Committee members were bewildered and not a little annoyed at the mass of rambling non sequiturs Budenz spewed forth.

It turned out, however, that Owen Lattimore's attorneys had brought along a surprise of their own. This was a deposition on the part of Dr. Bella V. Dodd, another ex-Communist who had once been a member of the Party's executive committee. In it she stated: "I have never met Owen Lattimore. I had never heard of him until the present controversy. In all my association with the Communist Party I never heard his name mentioned by Party leaders or friends of the Party. . . ."

McCarthy's case against Owen Lattimore, for the moment at least, remained a shambles. Having come up to bat three times and struck out three times, the senator from Wisconsin might well have contented himself with a return to the minor leagues. But his combative instincts and the enormous amount of publicity he was receiving persuaded him to continue the attack.

Beginning with his first "disclosures," McCarthy had insisted that "proof" of his charges could be found in the government's loyalty board files. As we have seen, President Truman had long since ordered that these files—containing, as they did, all sorts of unfounded, unproved and unevaluated information regarding the private lives of government employees—should remain closed to the public and to Congress. This, of course, provided instant ammunition to McCarthy and to those Republican senators willing to justify his activities. The files were closed, they charged, because they obviously contained information that would reveal that the Democratic administrations of Presidents Roosevelt and Truman had indeed been "soft on Communists." Senator Tydings and the Democrats serving on his subcommittee sought to quiet the uproar by eliciting statements from Attorney General McGrath and FBI Director J. Edgar Hoover, both of whom declared it would be "unthinkable" to release the files. This testimony from the arch-conservative guardians of the government's police power did not, however, soothe the outraged feelings of the Republicans. Seeing that McCarthy's allegations had so far failed to provide the political ammunition they sought, members of the Republican Senate Policy Committee decided to reap what political harvest they could from the "secret files" issue. At one time they seriously considered serving a subpoena on President Truman to force him to open the files. When the president declared he would accept no such subpoena, this tactic was dropped. Yet before the winds of rhetoric issuing from Capitol Hill, President Truman finally gave in. On May 4 he declared that the Tydings Committee could have access to the files of all eighty-one of the persons accused by Senator McCarthy.

Minute examination of these files revealed not one single fact upon which McCarthy's charges and innuendoes could seriously be based. And here, it would seem, was final and total defeat for Tail-Gunner Joe. Yet Senator Tydings and his colleagues did not reckon with McCarthy's large reserves of mendacity. When informed that the files contained nothing that would substantiate his allegations, Joe McCarthy simply declared that the files had been "raped"; they had been "skeletonized or tampered with." J. Edgar

Hoover himself declared that the files were complete and untampered with. But by that time Joe McCarthy was already attacking on another front, producing more verbiage, more headlines so bold as to bury his previous defeats from public view.

CHAPTER SIX

The Fall of the Mighty

What is there here other than a fraud and a hoax? It ought to make every American's blood boil that they have been told these foul charges.

—Sen. Millard Tydings (d., md.)

I hold myself accountable . . . first to the people of my state, and secondly to the people of the nation, and thirdly to civilization as a whole.

—Sen. Joseph R. McCarthy (r., wis.)

It might be supposed that the collapse of McCarthy's sensational charges under the scrutiny of the Tydings subcommittee would have left the senator isolated. Could even such professional Menace peddlers as Hearst or Kohlberg or Fulton Lewis, Jr., afford to associate themselves with McCarthy's recklessness? Yes, they could —and for a very good and sufficient reason. For although McCarthy's statements had been exposed as lies before the Tydings subcommittee, they had, through constant and irresponsible iteration in the nation's press, assumed substance and weight before the general public. Denials never caught up with charges; exposures never overtook innuendoes. As has been pointed out, very large and influential segments of the press, controlled by veteran alarmists, unashamedly supported McCarthy and, if anything, exaggerated his charges. But even respectable and basically anti-McCarthy journals contributed to his increasing notoriety simply by clinging to the ancient journalistic adage that "news is news." With McCarthy's false statements evoking headlines from their competitors, the "liberal" press felt constrained to evaluate not the content but the newsworthiness of the senator's lies in the same way. Most Americans, before turning to the sports or comics, glanced at the headlines and rarely bothered to read (when and if it followed) the analysis. The nation, ill served by but utterly dependent (in those pre-television days) on its press, was left with the uneasy feeling that where so much smoke erupted from Capitol Hill there must be some fire. Perhaps McCarthy erred in one or more of his particular charges (few bothered to satisfy themselves about this), but there *had* to be something to them; else what was all the shouting about? This was sufficient to create an atmosphere in which McCarthy's various backers could advance their own particular interests, be they paranoid-emotional (such as the wished-for reversal of history in the Far East), financial (the journalistic rewards to be reaped by sensation-mongering), or political (the destruction of the Truman administration). The overall technique employed consciously or otherwise by McCarthy, his backers and their allies or dupes among the mass media was one invented years before by Adolf Hitler's propaganda minister, Joseph Goebbels—the Big Lie technique. It consisted very simply of telling lies so obviously outrageous that those who heard them, even if they suspected their probity, would be bound to suppose that they reflected at least a bit of truth.

Far from becoming isolated, McCarthy, having proved himself a master at manipulating press publicity, now drew upon new sources of support. One of these was the wealth of Joseph P. Kennedy, who helped to finance much McCarthy publicity and also contributed to the senator's reelection campaign. Later, one of the Kennedy clan, young Robert F. Kennedy, was to join McCarthy's investigative staff, and his brother John F. Kennedy, newly elected to Congress, made a point during his congressional career of not attacking his colleague from Wisconsin.

Another and far more important new source of support now came from much of the hierarchy of the Catholic church in America. This religious backing was of supreme importance to McCarthy because it provided him with a cloak of respectability that he would otherwise have lacked. And this cloak covered neatly the naked immorality of McCarthy's tactics. For even if one believed implicitly in the senator's accusations or the righteousness of his cause, there remained a very serious question as to whether McCarthy's ends justified his means. These means were now known to include the theft of government documents, the subornation of perjury, and slander, at the very least. Yet for many important Catholic prelates, McCarthy's self-proclaimed ends (the defense of the republic against the Menace) justified these means. The story is told of a distinguished medieval prelate who, when asked if all the inhabitants of a besieged "heretical" city ought to be burned (a few of the faithful might thus also have been singed), replied: "Burn them all. God will know His own!" New York's Cardinal Spellman unconsciously echoed the views of his predecessor when he declared: ". . . The anguished cries and protests against 'McCarthyism' are not going to dissuade Americans from their desire to see Communists exposed and removed from positions where they can carry out their nefarious plans. . . ."

But if the immorality of McCarthy's tactics did not trouble clerical heads, it troubled—and deeply—the consciences of some of his Republican senatorial colleagues. On June 1, 1950, Mrs. Margaret Chase Smith, Republican senator from Maine, presented to the Senate a "Declaration of Conscience" signed by herself and six other Senate Republicans. Standing directly in front of McCarthy (who shielded his face with his hand), Mrs. Smith pointed out that the nation was "being psychologically divided by the confusions and suspicions that are bred in the United States Senate to spread like cancerous tentacles of 'know nothing, suspect everything' attitudes. . . .

"As a United States senator," she declared, "I am not proud of the way in which the Senate has been made a publicity platform for irresponsible sensationalism. I am not proud of the reckless abandon in which unproved charges have been hurled. . . ."

The senator from Maine said she did not want her party to win by riding "to political victory on the Four Horsemen of Calumny—Fear, Ignorance, Bigotry and Smear. . . . While it might be a fleeting victory for the Republican Party, it would be a more lasting defeat for the American people. . . ."

The Republican senators who joined Mrs. Smith in her Declaration of Conscience were Charles W. Tobey of New Hampshire; George D. Aiken of Vermont; Wayne L. Morse of Oregon; Irving

Senator Margaret Chase Smith, Maine Republican whose "Declaration of Conscience" sounded an early trumpet against McCarthyism. Few of her colleagues in either party had the courage openly to support her.

M. Ives of New York; Edward J. Thye of Minnesota; and Robert C. Hendrickson of New Jersey.

While Mrs. Smith received the congratulations of her colleagues, both Democratic and Republican, Senator McCarthy slunk from the Senate chamber. Yet the very next day he had recovered sufficiently to tell the Senate: "Let me make it clear to the administration, to the Senate and to the country that this fight against communism . . . shall not stop, regardless of what any group in this Senate or in the administration may do. . . ."

The truth was that despite their congratulations to Mrs. Smith, most Senate Republicans could not now afford to abandon their colleague from Wisconsin. There were some among them, like Bourke Hickenlooper, who were outright supporters of McCarthy's methods, but most preferred to support him from a safe distance. It was by now apparent that the Tydings Committee report, which would soon be submitted to the Senate, would become the center of a strictly political, strictly partisan battle royal. The report would show that McCarthy had lied, purely and simply. But its implications reached far beyond that. For if McCarthy had lied, then what about those Senate Republicans who had supported him openly or covertly? If he had lied, then perhaps the entire hullabaloo about "Communists in government," the whole Menace package, was a fraud. But the Republican Party had staked its hopes of winning both the 1950 midterm elections and the 1952 presidential election on convincing the American people that their Democratic government was riddled with spies and saboteurs and had been for years "soft on traitors." Their only hope, in the face of the damning evidence contained in the Tydings Committee report, would be to condemn the hearings in their entirety as a whitewash of the administration and an undeserved attack upon the Wisconsin senator.

For the Democrats, on the other hand, the Tydings Committee report would offer an opportunity both to attack Republican accusations and to "clear" their own party from mounting public suspicion. Congressional Democrats had been on the defensive ever since the conviction of Alger Hiss. They had seemed to lose faith in their own administration and, perhaps, faith in themselves. Nor were they united. For many Southern Democrats fully shared Republican antipathy to the liberal Truman administration, whereas Democrats from all sections of the country, as deluded regarding the limits of American power as their constituents, silently wondered if perhaps it *was,* after all, the fault of Democratic administrations that China had gone Communist. Yet the Tydings Committee report offered them one last chance to unite, both on principle and politically, to put an end to the mounting public hysteria that threatened them.

Then, on June 24 (Washington time), came a new shock. North Korean Communist armies invaded the Republic of South Korea, brushing aside disorganized resistance on the part of the South Korean army and its American advisers. That this invasion was but the climax of months of mutual provocations and border incidents in which both Koreas were equally guilty, that the Republic of South Korea was a dictatorship—all of this was ignored. A client of the United States had been attacked and American personnel were being killed. It was all true, then. There was a worldwide

Communist plot to conquer the free world through force of arms. (No one would believe that the North Koreans had attacked without the encouragement and backing of their patron, the Soviet Union.) This could well be the beginning of World War III—and the climate of public fear regarding the Menace reached the boiling point. It did not matter that the Truman administration hastily dispatched reinforcements to South Korea and committed the nation to war against this Communist attack; it did not matter that the United States (largely through canny maneuvering on the part of the administration) was joined by most of the members of the United Nations in its attempt to suppress this aggression. Americans were being killed by Communists, and somehow the Democrats were to blame.

Perhaps, in the long run, given the nature of American politics, the opportunity given to the Republican Party in 1950 was too great to be spurned. The Republicans had not, after all, elected a president since 1928; they had controlled Congress for only two of the previous twenty-two years; finally, they had been administered a shattering defeat in 1948 by Harry S Truman, in spite of the fact that the Democratic Party was split three ways that year. There were not a few Republicans who seriously believed that their party might become extinct if it did not soon win a national election. In any event, when the Tydings Committee report was brought before the Senate on July 17, 1950, Republicans labeled it a whitewash of the State Department and the administration and an unfair attack on Senator Joseph R. McCarthy.

The report was, of course, a total and complete denunciation of the falsity of McCarthy's charges and the unethical nature of his tactics. It took up the senator's allegations case by case and then demonstrated that there was no evidence to support any of them, not a single one. In a partisan fury, the Tydings Committee itself had split on the report. The Democrats issued the majority report while Senators Lodge and Hickenlooper issued a minority report. But even Senator Lodge's minority report did not support McCarthy. It simply insisted: "The fact that many charges have been made which have not been proved does not in the slightest degree relieve the subcommittee of the responsibility for undertaking a relentlessly thorough investigation of its own." Although how much more thorough the committee could have been was difficult to see.

Floor debate on the Tydings Committee report erupted on July 20, 1950. Tydings himself led the attack and spared McCarthy nothing. He accused the Wisconsin senator of resorting to "mud, slime and filth" in uttering his "foul and vile charges." But Senator Robert A. Taft ("Mr. Republican") leaped up to denounce the report as "derogatory and insulting to Senator McCarthy." Neither he nor any of the other Republican senators attempted to defend their colleague directly; instead they concentrated their fire on the report itself, insisting again and again that it was a "cover-up." At one point tempers were so strained that it seemed as if Senator Tydings and Republican Senator William E. Jenner of Indiana would come to blows. In the end, the Senate voted to accept the report—but on strict partisan lines.

As for McCarthy, the supposed victim of the report, he announced that "The most loyal stooges of the Kremlin could not have done a better job of giving a clean bill of health to Stalin's fifth column in this country. At a time when American blood is staining the Korean valleys, the Tydings-McMahon report gives unlimited aid and comfort to the very enemies responsible for tying the hands and shooting the faces off some of our soldiers."

The Hearst press was quick to support this conclusion. "As a public paper prepared in parlous times, it [the report] verges upon DISLOYALTY!" thundered the New York *Journal-American* editorially. All the professional Menace peddlers rushed into print to attack the report and defend McCarthy. And, in the climate of crisis provoked by the Korean War, many Americans accepted their views. How many, in any event, would actually read the report? How many had followed detail by detail the tortuous testimony that refuted McCarthy's charges? The technique of the Big Lie worked wonderfully against the Tydings Committee report; truth never did catch up to it. In the end, almost all observers were forced to agree that the weight of this investigation and denunciation of the Wisconsin senator's charges, ethics and tactics, which in normal times would have destroyed a senatorial reputation, had only enhanced his power and prestige.

Ironically, the man most hurt by the Tydings Committee report was Senator Millard Tydings himself—elegant, conservative, four times elected from his home state of Maryland, a political figure seemingly unassailable in his own bailiwick—for McCarthy was determined to have his revenge.

It so happened that Senator Tydings was standing for reelection in the fall of 1950. He was opposed by an all but unknown Republican candidate named John Marshall Butler. Sometime in July 1950 (after the Tydings Committee report had been made public), candidate Butler and his campaign manager appeared in McCarthy's office in Washington. They hinted that by helping Butler, McCarthy could have his revenge on Tydings. McCarthy enthusiastically accepted this open invitation to inject himself into Maryland politics and rounded up considerable financial and staff support for Butler. He elicited funds from such people as Texas millionaire Clint ("Only good red is one that's dead") Murchison, his friend H. L. ("I don't have no truck with com-symps") Hunt, Alfred (China Lobby) Kohlberg, and others of the extreme-right intelligentsia. McCarthy agent Don Surine was "loaned" to Butler for the duration.

One of the tactics used in the campaign against Senator Tydings was the distribution of 500,000 copies of a four-page tabloid entitled, portentously, *From the Record*. Sample headlines from this journal included such titles as: "TYDINGS BLAMED FOR HIGH KOREAN CASUALTIES"; "TYDINGS HELD UP ARMS FOR SOUTH KOREA, etc. Featured also in the tabloid was a faked photograph of Senator Tydings apparently deep in conversation with ex-Communist Party chief Earl Browder. The caption of this fraudulent photo read: "Communist leader Earl Browder, shown at left in this composite picture, was a star witness at the Tydings Committee hearings and was cajoled into saying that Owen Lattimore and others accused of disloyalty were not Communists. Tydings (left) answered, 'Oh, thank you, sir.' Browder testified in the best interests of those accused, naturally." The authors of the caption safeguarded themselves by the use of the word "composite" in describing the photo. But how many readers caught this distinction? Evidently not very many, for when the votes were counted, the veteran Millard Tydings had been beaten by more than 45,000—by a political unknown.

This paste-up job (produced by McCarthy's staff) helped defeat Millard Tydings in his bid for reelection in 1952. To the left (where else?) stands former Communist Party leader Earl Browder. He appears to be whispering secret instructions (direct from Moscow, no doubt) to the Maryland senator. The "photo" was, of course, a complete fake.

Nor was Tydings the only victim of McCarthy's fury that fall. Senator Scott Lucas, the Democratic majority leader from Illinois, being opposed for the Senate by Republican Everett McKinley Dirksen, also lost badly—after McCarthy had campaigned vigorously against him in Illinois. In Idaho and Utah too McCarthy's support seemed decisive in the election of two new Republican senators. The lesson was clear: with McCarthy's support you won; against him you lost.

The lesson may have been clear, but it was extremely misleading. Detailed analysis of the Illinois campaign, for example, later demonstrated that Scott Lucas had been defeated on a variety of issues, most of them purely local. Yet a legend had been born, and it certainly seemed substantiated by the results of the Maryland election.

The means by which that election had been won were not simply unethical; some of them were even illegal under Maryland law. On the basis of these illegalities, Senator Tydings asked the Senate to investigate the election to see whether Senator-elect Butler was qualified to take his Senate seat. The investigation was turned over to the Elections Subcommittee of the Senate Rules Committee. The subcommittee was headed by Senator Guy M. Gillette (D., Iowa), and its other members included Democrats A.S. (Mike) Monroney of Oklahoma and Thomas Hennings of Missouri, and Republicans Robert C. Hendrickson of New Jersey and Margaret Chase Smith of Maine. The two Republican senators, be it noted, had been signers of Mrs. Smith's Declaration of Conscience a few months before.

The Gillette committee found ample evidence to warrant a scathing indictment of the means used to defeat Senator Tydings; it found reason to suggest that McCarthy agent Don Surine be indicted for perjury; it found that specific Maryland laws had been broken by Butler's staff; it suggested that the Senate might consider unseating McCarthy himself for his role in the campaign; and it found that, despite all the evidence under existing Senate rules, *there were no grounds for unseating Senator-elect Butler.*

What was Joe McCarthy's reaction? "As long as puny politicians try to encourage other puny politicians to ignore or whitewash Communist influences in our government," Joe warned, "America will remain in grave danger."

That McCarthy was still manning the barricades to avert this "grave danger" became apparent during the first months of 1951 when he injected himself into the "Rosenberg affair." At the request of Secretary of Defense George C. Marshall, Mrs. Anna Rosenberg, a well-known businesswoman from New York and an expert in the field of manpower utilization, had been nominated by President Truman as an assistant secretary in the Department of Defense. On November 29, 1950, the Senate Armed Services Committee unanimously endorsed the appointment. But in the meantime a campaign against Mrs. Rosenberg's nomination was being organized by such notorious anti-Semites as Gerald L. K. Smith and Benjamin Freedman. They were abetted by Hearst Menace expert J. B. Matthews and radio commentator Fulton Lewis, Jr. These men were quite certain that Mrs. Rosenberg was a Communist. They based their assertion on the testimony of one Ralph DeSola, an ex-Communist turned government informer and an employee of

Alfred Kohlberg. In early December 1950 Freedman, armed with credentials from Fulton Lewis, Jr., along with Gerald L. K. Smith spent a day rushing around Washington buttonholing representatives and senators to urge that Mrs. Rosenberg's nomination be blocked. It is some measure of the atmosphere prevalent in Washington at that time that this group of shabby fanatics succeeded. Alarmed at the mounting pressure, the Senate Armed Services Committee hastily met to announce that it would "reconsider" the Rosenberg appointment.

Meanwhile, scenting publicity, Senator McCarthy had entered the fray. He sent his super-sleuth Don Surine, along with Edward K. Nellor (another super-sleuth from the offices of Fulton Lewis, Jr.), to see Mr. Freedman. The two agents came armed with a letter of introduction from Gerald L. K. Smith which began: "Congratulations on the terrific job you are doing in helping to keep the Zionist Jew Anna M. Rosenberg from becoming the director of the Pentagon. This is to introduce two gentlemen who are helping in this fight. . . ." Surine and Nellor were sent by Freedman to interview Ralph DeSola, and it was speedily arranged that DeSola would testify against Mrs. Rosenberg.

On December 8, 1950, DeSola told the assembled Senate Armed Services Committee that he knew Mrs. Rosenberg was a Communist. Witnesses, he said, would support his statement. In a dramatic face-to-face confrontation he positively identified Mrs. Rosenberg as the Anna Rosenberg he had met in 1934 at a gathering of the John Reed Club (an avowedly Communist group). Mrs. Rosenberg's response was very direct. "He is a liar," she told the committee. "I would like to lay my hands on that man." But there was more anguish than anger in her testimony.

"I tried to think," she said: "Where do I know this man? How do I know him from someplace? How can a human being do this to someone? What can he have against me? I don't know him. . . . I plead with you to finish this. If you don't think I'm fit to take this office, say so. I don't care what you charge me with, but not disloyalty, Senator. It is an awful thing to carry around with you."

Fortunately for Mrs. Rosenberg, the full research resources of the Pentagon were now employed in her behalf. It soon developed that there was another Anna Rosenberg, then living in California, who had indeed been a member of the John Reed Club in 1934 and perhaps was the Anna Rosenberg to whom DeSola referred. Furthermore, DeSola's witnesses, instead of verifying his testimony, utterly repudiated it. The case against Mrs. Rosenberg collapsed and her appointment to the Department of Defense was again confirmed (with even genial Joe McCarthy now voting in her favor). It would seem that the matter was nothing more than a misguided tempest in the mind of a crackpot.

But it was a highly instructive tempest. For this infamous "Rosenberg affair" very aptly reflected the nightmare atmosphere that was beginning to build in Washington. First of all, there was the amazing spectacle of a Senate committee rushing to "reconsider" its recommendation on the basis of lobbying conducted by such shabby types as Freedman and Gerald L. K. Smith (leader of the Fascist "American Christian Crusade"). Secondly, there was the curious fact that Ralph DeSola, who had committed perjury when he identified Mrs. Rosenberg face to face, was never prosecuted. But such procedure was in accordance with standard government practice. None of the government informers, ex-Communists, or self-powered Menace peddlers such as DeSola, Louis Budenz, Don Surine and Whittaker Chambers were ever prosecuted for the many misstatements they made under oath. In the prevailing atmosphere of paranoid suspicion and fear, the government felt it had to protect its spies and informers at all costs—including the cost of destroying innocent reputations and making a mockery of the law. Finally, the Rosenberg case demonstrated the increasing power of Joe McCarthy. After all, the Senate Armed Services Committee had heeded the tales of Freedman and Gerald L. K. Smith in the first place, vicious as they were, only because they had emerged from and were coordinated by Senator McCarthy's office. And once again, despite the humiliating debacle to which the charges against Mrs. Rosenberg led, Tail-Gunner Joe emerged from the matter unscathed. Neither in the Senate nor in the nation's press was his part in this shameful episode denounced.

In a sense, a politician's power may be measured by the enemies he is willing to make, and nothing better illustrated the increasing power of Senator Joseph R. McCarthy than his attack on George Catlett Marshall, which he delivered in a set speech on the floor of the Senate on June 14, 1951.

In choosing George C. Marshall for his target, McCarthy revealed remarkable impudence. It was Chief of Staff Marshall whose brilliant military strategies had guided American and British forces to victory in World War II; while he was secretary of state he had originated the Marshall Plan through which shattered Europe's economy had been rebuilt; he was now serving as secretary of defense during the perilous times of the Korean War. His entire life had been dedicated in a singularly selfless way to the service of his country. He had never sought public office but had accepted it when his country needed him. In the manner of Dwight Eisenhower or Douglas MacArthur, he had never placed much value on public acclaim. Washington correspondent Richard Rovere described him:

". . . It was not so much what he had done as what he was and what he symbolized that made so many stand in awe of him. He was, above all, a man of vast and palpable dignity. The dignity was in his bearing and in his entire mien, in his aloofness from controversy, in the silence with which he had borne disappointment and defeat and sorrow, with which he was well acquainted. He was the very image of the strong, noble, gentle Southern man of arms who could be no more dishonored by enemies and critics, if he had any, than the great progenitor of the tradition, Marshall's fellow Virginian Robert E. Lee."

McCarthy's attack on Marshall was prompted not only by a desire to link his name, even in this scurrilous manner, with the person many had called "the Greatest Living American." It was at least partly inspired by the tactical necessity of pushing himself once more into the headlines. For the last few weeks McCarthy's news value had been usurped by an event that rendered the Wisconsin senator's accusations all but insignificant as news copy. This event was President Truman's recall of General Douglas MacArthur from his position as Supreme Commander of the Allied Forces in Japan and his dismissal as Commander of the United Nations Forces in Korea. Truman's decision to fire MacArthur, a public hero in his own right, was based on several reasons, of which the overriding one was the fundamental American principle that the military is, and must be, subordinate to the civilian government. MacArthur had been so flagrantly insubordinate as to leave the president very little choice. Defense Secretary Marshall supported the president's decision. Republican senators, scenting the possibility that MacArthur might make a popular presidential candidate in 1952, invited the general to testify before the full Armed Services Committee. And these were the hearings that had driven McCarthy's name from the headlines. By attacking Marshall, McCarthy was, in a sense, injecting himself into the controversy.

The speech through which Joe McCarthy attempted to destroy George Marshall's reputation was delivered only in part (after reading the first 20,000 words McCarthy wearily inserted the remaining 40,000 into the *Congressional Record*) before a nearly empty Senate. The manuscript from which he read, with its many historical allusions, its didactic tone and its impeccable literacy, was certainly not the work of Tail-Gunner Joe. It has been suggested that the speech was concocted by historians at Georgetown University, or at least by men under their influence. This suggestion is based on the fact that the analysis of contemporary history contained in the speech is totally "revisionist," and Georgetown University was, as it remains, the seat of this remarkable view of world events.

To revisionist historians almost all the works and decisions of most American leaders have been in error since 1932 (the year of Franklin Roosevelt's election). This is true because, since 1917, there has never been more than one genuine threat to the world, and that threat is embodied in the Soviet Union and the world Communist movement. Hence, any decisions which have advanced the power of the Communist world, no matter why they were made, were wrong and possibly subversive. This view totally ignores, of course, the very real threat to the world posed by Hitler's nazism and Italian fascism during the thirties and forties. It suggests that the United States was fighting the wrong countries during the Second World War. It insists that Roosevelt never should have sent military aid to Russia when she was invaded by Germany in 1941; that American military leaders should have concentrated their efforts on preventing Russian expansion into the Balkans during the war rather than assaulting Germany directly on the western front; and that Russia never should have been invited to enter the war against Japan.

These opinions take no notice of the fact that, had Russia been defeated by the Germans (as she might well have been without American aid), the United States, at the cost of innumerable American lives, might have had to face Hitler's hordes alone. They overlook the fact that had not Allied armies struck directly against Germany, Nazi scientists might have had the time needed to perfect their rocketry and jet aircraft and perhaps to unlock the secrets of the atomic bomb. They ignore the testimony of military experts that an invasion of Japan (which might have been necessary without Russian intervention) would have cost at least a million American casualties. They ignore the testimony of defeated Japanese leaders themselves who declared that it was Russian intervention and not the use of the atomic bomb which finally resulted in their decision to surrender. In short, although seemingly more "informed," the revisionist view of history is not dissimilar to the paranoid interpretation of history discussed earlier in this book.

George Catlett Marshall had been associated, of course, with almost all the important decisions formulated by American policy makers during the late thirties and forties. Therefore he was guilty. Guilty of being mistaken? No; along with almost all high American leaders, guilty of treason! The speech was specific about this. In part it read:

"How can we account for our present situation unless we believe that men high in this government are concerting to deliver us to disaster? This must be the product of a great conspiracy, a conspiracy on a scale so immense as to dwarf any previous such venture in the history of man. A conspiracy of infamy so black that, when it is finally exposed, its principals shall forever deserve the maledictions of all honest men. . . . What can be made of this unbroken series of decisions and acts contributing to the strategy of defeat? They cannot be attributed to incompetence. If Marshall were merely stupid, the laws of probability would dictate that part of his decisions would serve his country's interest."

Unbelievable though it may seem, this vituperative blast of ignorant hot air, this "patent medicine" speech, succeeded in driving George Marshall from public life. For although standing above and outside any political party, Marshall served in a Democratic administration. Yet not one voice was raised in his behalf on the floor of the Senate. No leading Democrats were willing to defend their own secretary of defense: McCarthy had succeeded in making a "controversial" figure of him. His usefulness was impaired. A few months after McCarthy's speech Marshall retired to private life. His departure left a vacancy on the American horizon that no man since has been big enough to fill.

How was it possible that McCarthy could get away with this infamous smear of a great American? The answer is a four-letter word: fear. His supposed political victories against Senators Tydings and Scott Lucas had left the rest of the Senate in mortal fear that one day he might invade their own states to assassinate their careers too. Outside the Senate, in the administration itself, that same four-letter word was operative. Not even President Harry S Truman, it seemed, was willing to tangle with Joe McCarthy.

It was not, of course, simply fear of the man himself or even of his political "savvy." It was a deep and unreasoning dread of the forces Joe McCarthy represented. It appeared that in 1951 a majority of the American people could no longer be reached by reason, that they had been "captured" by the Menace peddlers, that they were sick with that political paranoid fever that extreme rightists had been trying for so long to inject into the American body politic. To oppose Joe McCarthy, it was supposed, was to arouse the unreasoning suspicion and hate of so substantial a number of Americans as to commit political suicide.

A pathetic example of the reality behind this dread was provided by the fate of the distinguished Democratic senator from Connecticut, William Benton. Benton, long a critic of McCarthy, rose in the Senate on August 6, 1951, to introduce a resolution that the Senate Rules Committee examine the conduct of Joe McCarthy with a view to expelling him from the United States Senate. He based his resolution on the damning evidence contained in the Tydings Committee report and on other instances of misconduct.

Benton's fellow senators, appalled by his daring, rushed to take cover. Only Joe McCarthy had anything to say about the Benton resolution: "Benton today," he declared, "has performed the

The Gillette subcommittee considers the Benton resolution calling on the Senate to expel McCarthy in 1951. None of the subcommittee members appear overly enthusiastic about their task. Left to right: Senators Margaret Chase Smith (R., Maine); Guy M. Gillette, (D., Iowa), chairman; A. S. "Mike" Monroney (D., Okla.); Thomas C. Hennings, Jr. (D., Mo.); and subcommittee counsel John Moore.

important service of helping to properly label the administration branch of the Democratic party as the party which stands for government of, by and for Communists, crooks and cronies."

Senator Guy Gillette would once again have to preside over this investigation, and he was openly reluctant to do so. He declared that the committee would hear Benton's charges and then decide if any further action was to be taken. Accordingly, on September 28, 1951, Benton appeared before the committee and read a scathing denunciation of Senator Joseph McCarthy. After reviewing his career and accusing him (with documentation) of graft, corruption and slander, Benton closed: "I submit that there is one act of hypocrisy which most offends the deepest convictions of the Christian conscience and also the American spirit of justice and fair play. That act is to put the brand of guilt upon an innocent man."

But evidently neither the Christian conscience nor the American spirit of justice and fair play was at home that day. Senator Gillette remarked that there would be some delay before his committee could decide whether or not to investigate Benton's charges. Not for several weeks would this reluctant committee get to work. When it did, it displayed a groveling fear of Joe McCarthy. For example, on nine different occasions the Gillette committee pleaded with McCarthy to appear before it and present his side of the story. But the senator contemptuously refused. Replying to one such invitation from Gillette, he wrote: "Frankly, Guy, I have not and do not intend to even read, much less answer, Benton's smear attack. . . ."

And so the investigation dragged on for a year and a half. During its course McCarthy attacked the committee in the usual ways, implying that its members were Communist stooges who were guilty of "recklessly wasting" the public's money. He also attacked Benton himself, accusing him of graft and of Communist leanings. The committee defended itself as best it could, avoiding any overly inquisitive probings into Joe McCarthy's political and financial transactions; it investigated and then cleared Senator Benton and finally, in January of 1953, brought in a report which (like others before it) condemned the Wisconsin senator. No action was ever taken as a result of this report.

As for Senator Benton, this lonely crusader brought down upon his own head the full force of McCarthy's wrath. Benton was standing for reelection in 1952, and McCarthy did not fail to invade his state to declare: "Joe Stalin could not have had a top agent in the United States who could have done a better job than Benton has done." In the end Benton went down to defeat, and once again the fearful lesson that it was political suicide to oppose Joe McCarthy was driven home to politicians across the land. An analysis of the Connecticut election would demonstrate that McCarthy's campaigning against Benton had had little effect on the outcome—but that analysis would come much later.

Senators Lucas, Tydings and Benton; General of the Army George Catlett Marshall—these mighty figures had been toppled by McCarthy. But the year 1952 was to provide an even greater victory for Tail-Gunner Joe.

Nineteen hundred fifty-two was a presidential election year. That year the Democrats nominated Governor Adlai E. Stevenson of Illinois to oppose the Republican candidate, General Dwight D.

Eisenhower. McCarthy himself was up for reelection in Wisconsin —and he won handily (such were the fruits of that lunch at the Colony restaurant when Joe had been searching for a "cause"), but, of greater importance, he and his tactics were to be used on the national level by the Republican Campaign Committee. Thus the nation was treated to the spectacle of McCarthy shouting that he wished "for a club to teach little Ad-lie patriotism." He further entertained with a long and rambling television speech, packed with lies and innuendoes, during which he attempted to prove that Adlai Stevenson was "a dupe of the Kremlin." All of this might well have been expected. Since Adlai Stevenson stood almost no chance of defeating Dwight Eisenhower, McCarthy's contributions to the campaign hardly seemed to matter.

But there was another incident connected with the 1952 presidential campaign that illustrated, on a very basic level, the depths into which American political life had been plunged. This incident may well be seen as McCarthy's greatest victory. Dwight David Eisenhower was a lifelong personal friend of General George Catlett Marshall. It was to Marshall that Eisenhower owed his rapid advancement before and during World War II. It was Marshall who had chosen Ike to command the North African invasion and later named him Supreme Commander of the Allied Expeditionary Force in western Europe. Would Eisenhower, who presented himself to the nation as a model of honor and righteousness, take the occasion of his campaign appearance in Wisconsin to defend his old friend and mentor after McCarthy's scurrilous attack? It would seem that Eisenhower could lose nothing by such a defense of George Marshall: his election was all but certain anyhow. And, be it said to Eisenhower's credit, he did intend to pay a personal tribute to Marshall in Milwaukee, right in McCarthy's backyard. His prepared speech included these lines:

". . . The right to question a man's judgment carries with it no automatic right to question his honor.

"Let me be quite specific. I know that charges of disloyalty, in the past, have been leveled against General George C. Marshall. I have been privileged for thirty-five years to know General Marshall personally. I know him, as a man and as a soldier, to be dedicated with singular selflessness and the profoundest patriotism to the service of America."

Although his tribute to Marshall was mild and his criticism of McCarthy implied rather than direct, the Wisconsin senator, learning what Eisenhower planned to say, was disturbed. Reportedly he made a secret visit to Eisenhower's campaign headquarters and demanded that the offending paragraph be deleted from the speech.

And the man who had presided over the Allied victory in Europe, the man who had been president of Columbia University, the man who was soon to be president of the United States, gave in. The references to Marshall were eliminated from the speech, and Eisenhower personally appeared with McCarthy in Wisconsin, remarking that he was for "good Republican candidates everywhere."

The personal shame that remained was Dwight D. Eisenhower's; the political shame remained with every American.

Having abandoned his old friend and patron George C. Marshall to "red scare" slander, candidate Dwight D. Eisenhower shakes hands with the chief slanderer in Milwaukee during the presidential campaign of 1952. Beaming his approval on this spectacle is the local Republican Party county chairman.

CHAPTER SEVEN

The Senator Becomes
an Ism

This committee isn't set up to show that agencies are
doing what they're supposed to do. Our job is to find the
weak spots.

—ROY COHN

McCarthy's realm is often described as the place where
men are held to be guilty until they prove their
innocence. But now I can personally report that it is also
a place where the existence of proof of innocence
becomes damning evidence of guilt.

—JAMES A. WECHSLER

MORE THAN a few Americans voted for Dwight D. Eisenhower in
1952 precisely because they believed that a Republican presidential
victory would result in the muffling of Joe McCarthy. There were
reasonable grounds for such a belief. After all, the entire purpose of
the McCarthy witch hunt had been a Republican victory at the
polls; with this achieved, why bother to continue? Would a
Republican senator seek the destruction of a Republican administration? Furthermore, Dwight D. Eisenhower was a political figure
of awesome proportions, the very father-image in whose arms
Americans yearned to sleep through the irritating problems of the
next four years. He had intimated that he was far above the
political fray, and he had let it be known that he personally
detested Joe McCarthy. True, he had had to deny his convictions
on that black day in Wisconsin when he had "chickened out" on

General Marshall. But now that he was safely elected, he would surely swat the Wisconsin gadfly should that insect attempt to sting him or his administration. On a deeper level, perhaps this first presidential election victory since 1928 would soothe the fears and ease the hysteria of those Republicans who in their desperation had embraced the Menace as the only available road back to power.

Those Americans who calculated thus made several grievous errors. First of all, they overlooked the fact that McCarthy was an independent demagogue; he was not beholden to the Republican Party for his prestige, and his prestige could only be maintained by a continuing diet of sensational news breaks, which could only come from further attacks on the United States government: there was no other source for McCarthy. Secondly, they overestimated the moral courage of Dwight D. Eisenhower, just as they overrated his political acumen. And, finally, they failed to see that the whirlwind of hysteria created by nearly a decade of Menace peddling had generated emotions too strong to be diminished by mere political victory.

Riding the shirttails of the Eisenhower landslide, the Republicans won control of both houses of Congress in 1952. And when the new Congress convened in January of 1953 it was the Republican leadership that now assigned committee posts. As a reward for McCarthy's considerable services during the campaign, the Republicans named the Wisconsin senator chairman of the Senate Committee on Government Operations. But there was more to this reward than met the eye, for this particular committee, though powerful, was supposed to concern itself with such dull matters as overseeing the operations of various government departments, reorganizing bureaus, auditing finances, and investigating graft. Membership on the Senate Internal Security Committee, which devoted itself to protecting America from the Menace, was denied to McCarthy. His Republican colleagues apparently felt that Tail-Gunner Joe had been throttled by this "reward." "We've got McCarthy where he can't do any harm," said Senator Robert A. Taft.

But once again his colleagues underrated Joe McCarthy. Within a very short time the genie was out of the bottle. An examination of the structure of the Senate Committee on Government Operations revealed to McCarthy's practiced eye a shining possibility. This possibility lay in the Permanent Subcommittee on Investigations, which, though supposedly concerned with the exposure of corruption in government, really had the potential power to investigate almost anything. McCarthy immediately named himself chairman of this permanent subcommittee and disregarded his duties as chairman of the parent Committee on Government Operations. Under his leadership, he was certain, the permanent subcommittee would soon steal the spotlight from all rival investigating committees.

To help him in his continuing crusade McCarthy now hired two young men (both twenty-six) who would soon become notorious as the most comically sinister vaudeville team ever to perform on the American political stage: Roy M. Cohn and G. David Schine (chanted reporters: "Absolutely, Mr. Cohn? Positively, Mr. Schine!")

Roy Cohn, who was hired as chief counsel to McCarthy's permanent subcommittee, had been something of a prodigy. He had received his law degree from Columbia University at the age of nineteen and soon after became a confidential assistant to the U.S. attorney for the Southern District of New York. Displaying fiery zeal and tremendous energy, Cohn plunged into the investigation and prosecution of all sorts of underworld malfeasance. Later he assisted in the prosecution of Julius and Ethel Rosenberg and of the leaders of the Communist Party. It seemed to many observers that his lust to defend the republic was matched only by his lust for personal glorification. In many ways he was not unlike his boss, Joe McCarthy.

G. David Schine, the scion of a hotel-chain owner, had less impressive credentials for the post of chief consultant to which he was appointed by McCarthy. He had dabbled in his father's hotel business, had been a press agent for Vaughn Monroe's orchestra, had dated several Hollywood starlets, and had authored a remarkable six-page pamphlet entitled "Definition of Communism" which was placed on the bedside tables in his father's hotels. The pamphlet was remarkable for its errors, both factual and substantive. It misdated such events as the Russian Revolution and the founding of the Communist Party; it misnamed such personalities

Backed by his trusty and world-renowned specialists in the theory and practice of Marxian dialectical materialism, G. David Schine and Roy M. Cohn, Chairman McCarthy of the Senate Permanent Subcommittee on Investigations prepares to dislodge the Communist witches from the Voice of America.

as Lenin; it confused other personalities such as Marx with Lenin and Stalin with Trotsky. It was also hopelessly confused in its interpretations. Yet this document served as G. David Schine's *bona fides* in the crusade against the Menace. In truth, if Schine had any occupation it was that of playboy.

Now, with the prodigy and the playboy to help him, McCarthy undertook to investigate Communist infiltration of the Voice of America, the radio propaganda instrument of the State Department's International Information Administration. As soon as the hearings opened on February 16, 1953, it became apparent that the core of McCarthy's charges had to do with a highly technical matter—the placement of the Voice's two powerful shortwave transmitters, Baker East and Baker West. These two radio transmitters (the most powerful in the world) had been built for the purpose of breaking through Russian "jamming" areas to deliver the Voice's message behind the Iron Curtain. The selection of their sites was obviously a vital matter, since some areas are much more subject to magnetic storms than others. To solve these and other problems the State Department had enlisted the help of the Massachusetts Institute of Technology, the Radio Corporation of America, the Bureau of Standards, and the U.S. Army Signal Corps. The experts, after much deliberation, agreed that Baker East should be located near Cape Hatteras and Baker West near Seattle, Washington.

Like any other large government agency, the Voice of America had not a few dissatisfied employees and harbored not a few interpersonal grudges and feuds. Now these disenchanted people paraded before the permanent subcommittee, where under the friendly prodding of Roy Cohn they hinted at dark and dangerous conspiracies at the Voice.

"As well as the question of waste," McCarthy asked one "cooperative" witness, "what other significance do you find in the location of Baker East and Baker West? . . . Assume I do not want that [voice] to reach Communist territory. Would not the best way to sabotage that voice be to place your transmitters within that magnetic storm area? . . . Now has it ever been suggested . . . that this mislocation of stations . . . has not been entirely the result of incompetence, but that some of it may have been purposely planned that way?"

Of course only the disaffected were invited to testify. None of the many experts, the overwhelming majority of whom approved of the locations of the two "Bakers," were heard. In one case, the views of an expert were totally distorted and misrepresented to make it appear that he backed up McCarthy's charges.

It might be assumed that the powerful new Republican administration would stand up to such ridiculous charges against what was now one of its own agencies. It did nothing of the kind. Instead, in the face of McCarthy's wild accusations (and the headlines they engendered), the State Department hurriedly scrapped the two transmitters and canceled the entire program. The Voice of America, it seemed, would not in fact reach beyond the Iron Curtain.

The Voice of America, it will be recalled, was no more than a subsidiary agency of the State Department's International Information Administration. This parent body also administered overseas

American libraries as part of its activities. As soon as McCarthy started his probe of VOA, Eisenhower's new secretary of state, John Foster Dulles, in a panic before the approach of the awesome inquisitors, hastily issued a directive that read as follows: "No material by any Communists, fellow-travelers, et cetera, will be used under any circumstances by any IIA media." When queried by stunned IIA administrators in the field whether this directive really meant what it seemed to mean, Dulles fired off a clarifying statement in which he ruled that the IIA must not use "*any* words for *any* purpose by a Communist or an 'et cetera.' "

In other words, Marx could not be quoted in order to be refuted; Lenin could not be quoted in order to be understood; Stalin could not be quoted in order to demonstrate that he had lied. And what about those "et ceteras"? Who were they?

Cohn and Schine were going to find out. They were going to find out and at the same time have a "swinging" European vacation at the taxpayers' expense. The prodigy and the playboy arrived in Paris on April 4, 1953. There they revealed to bemused European reporters that they had come to investigate the IIA's overseas libraries. For what? demanded the reporters. For inefficiency, replied Mr. Cohn. But inefficiency included subversion, clarified Mr. Schine. So the boys flitted around Europe (twelve capitals in seventeen days) pursued by a horde of reporters and photographers who found them the most amusing spectacle since the Congress of Vienna. One episode involved Mr. Schine chasing Mr. Cohn through a hotel lobby while swatting him soundly about the ears with a rolled-up magazine; another involved the coy way the two boys would ask for hotel rooms at their various stops. Since McCarthy had implied that the State Department was loaded with homosexuals, Mr. Cohn and Mr. Schine would demand separate but adjoining rooms and then (digging each other in the ribs jovially) explain to baffled hotel clerks: "You see, we *don't* work for the State Department."

In each of their target cities the pair would spend a few minutes going through the card index files of the local IIA overseas library. It was not sufficient that a library be untainted by the presence of "et cetera" works; it also had to be stocked with such tasteful examples of mid-century American writing as *The American Legion*

Magazine if its director was to avert the wrath of the new inquisitors. In Vienna, Mr. Cohn and Mr. Schine boldly sallied forth from the American sector to visit the Russian Cultural Center's rival library. There they found that this indisputably Communist organization harbored the works of Mark Twain. Armed with this information, the pair rushed back to the IIA library and there, sure enough, were the works of Mark Twain: proof positive that the Vienna branch of IIA was riddled with subversives and "et ceteras."

Mr. Cohn and Mr. Schine, having completed their investigations, returned home, leaving behind them the mocking laughter of a continent. But they left more than that in Europe. After all, the prodigy and the playboy *were* officially employed by the legislative branch of the government of the United States. What kind of government sent such idiots abroad? wondered many Europeans. The Cohn-Schine vaudeville junket in Europe undoubtedly did more damage to the reputation of the United States than years of Communist propaganda. It did much damage to the IIA's European program too. Many IIA personnel resigned in disgust; others determined to keep their mouths shut forever after—not precisely the role information officers ought to play.

Having drawn blood on the subject of writers through this European grand tour, Cohn and Schine, backed as always by McCarthy, now turned their attention to a "clean sweep" of American writers of suspect ideology. It had been discovered, McCarthy charged, that IIA libraries harbored works by many well-known Communists and "et ceteras." Who were they? Such authors as John Dewey, Henry Steele Commager, Bernard DeVoto, Louis Bromfield, Theodore Dreiser and Edna Ferber; novelist Sherwood Anderson and drama critic Brooks Atkinson; poets Archibald MacLeish, W. H. Auden and Stephen Vincent Benét. One of the names on the list was that of a close relative of Secretary of State Dulles, Foster Rhea Dulles. "Why," demanded the baffled secretary, "have they got my cousin on that list?"

No one ever told him why. It wasn't necessary. Crawling before the might of Joe McCarthy, the State Department hurriedly sent out orders that the works of all such writers, playwrights and poets (including the mystery novels of Dashiell Hammett) be banned. Accordingly, they were removed and hidden in basements. In some libraries (which perhaps did not have basements) books were burned. But this, decided John Foster Dulles, was going too far. Hitler's minions had burned books; Americans should never do that. So the actual burnings stopped, but not the bannings.

Perhaps shocked by this vivid reminder of the early days of nazism in the late unlamented Third Reich, President Eisenhower, addressing an audience of Dartmouth College students on June 14, 1953, pleaded: "Don't join the book-burners. . . . Don't be afraid to go to the library and read every book. . . ." Fitting advice from the soldier-hero president to a college audience, and totally indicative of the moral fortitude of the nation at that time. Yet, when rebuked by an enraged McCarthy, Eisenhower even retreated from that innocuous entreaty. He told reporters that he approved of the destruction of books that advocated the overthrow of the United States government by force and violence and that he had not been thinking specifically of Joe McCarthy when he made his speech.

The result? IIA was disbanded and a new organization, the United States Information Agency, was created to take its place. How powerful could the junior senator from Wisconsin become? It seemed that the Eisenhower administration was merely the errand boy of Tail-Gunner Joe.

Curiously enough, Tail-Gunner Joe was beginning to seem like the errand boy of Roy Cohn and his sidekick G. David Schine. In committee hearings observers noted that McCarthy took his cues from Cohn; increasingly, it seemed, he relied on the judgment of the prodigy and the playboy. This was bound to lead to disaster, and many wondered just what hold Mr. Cohn and Mr. Schine had over the senator.

Perhaps in an effort to bring his young assistants under control, but probably because he was impressed by the man himself, Joe McCarthy on June 22, 1953, appointed the dean of Menace peddlers, J. B. ("Doc") Matthews, as executive director of the permanent subcommittee's investigative staff. It will be recalled that this was the same Matthews who for many years had supplied the "intellectual" background for the Hearst press's anti-Communist crusades. It happened that Matthews's appointment coincided with the appearance in the July 1953 issue of *American Mercury* magazine of another red-baiting article by this learned man. In the article Matthews undertook to prove that the American Protestant clergy was riddled with and ruled by sinister agents of the Kremlin. "The largest single group supporting the Communist apparatus in the United States today is composed of Protestant clergymen," Matthews revealed. The Communist Party had "enlisted the support of at least 7,000 Protestant clergymen," as spies, dupes, saboteurs and trouble-makers.

And here at last, through an incredible miscalculation for so politically canny an operator, Joe McCarthy overstepped himself. He had attacked and degraded almost every aspect of American official life; he had vilified generals of the army, presidents and many lesser public servants. But he had never denounced God or womanhood or Mom's apple pie; these, after all, were sacred to every American. Now, however, by appointing the learned Matthews to a high post on his permanent subcommittee, McCarthy was backing the man who had labeled white Anglo-Saxon Protestant clergymen as *Reds!* It was not to be borne, not even by the craven Eisenhower administration. McCarthy, through Matthews, had stirred up the beehive, and the WASPs were out to sting him.

The sting was administered through a presidential statement which read in part: ". . . Generalized and irresponsible attacks that sweepingly condemn the whole of any group of citizens are alien to America. Such attacks betray contempt for the principles of freedom and decency. . . ." One wonders whether the generalized attacks upon that group of citizens known as Democrats ("the Party of treason," "the American Communist front," etc.) indulged in by McCarthy and Vice-President Richard M. Nixon also affronted Eisenhower's sense of decency. If so he never betrayed the fact.

However belated, nonetheless this statement was a severe rebuke. In effect Dwight D. Eisenhower was betting that his personal appeal to the American electorate outweighed that of McCarthy. The president was right. Not only that: McCarthy's defense of Matthews (whom he stubbornly wished to retain on the subcommittee) alienated even Republican senators from Bible-belt states, whose constituents were now writing angry letters about McCarthy's "attack on God."

Under pressure from fellow senators on the permanent subcommittee, McCarthy gave in and fired Matthews. But this was not enough for the Democratic members of the subcommittee (Senators Stuart Symington of Missouri, Henry M. Jackson of Washington and the veteran John L. McClellan of Arkansas), who now, scenting blood, demanded that McCarthy also fire Mr. Roy Cohn. But this was a step McCarthy would not take. As chairman of the permanent subcommittee, he declared that he had the sole right to hire and fire members of his staff. When he insisted on this position, the three Democrats on the subcommittee did something all but unheard of in senatorial annals: they simply walked away. On July 10, 1953, Senators Symington, Jackson, and McClellan declared they would have nothing further to do with the permanent subcommittee. Hence McCarthy's committee was left with only Republicans. The Democrats were pinning responsibility for Joe McCarthy where it properly belonged: on the Republican Party.

It was soon after this unexpected development that two important events occurred in Senator McCarthy's life. The first of these was the notification by the Selective Service Administration to Mr. G. David Schine that he would soon be inducted into the United States Army. Uncle Sam, it seemed, by drafting the redoubtable Schine (just like untold millions of other young men) would soon present him with an opportunity to defend the republic in a more concrete way than by harassing public servants. This event was to have vast ramifications. The second, happier, event in Senator McCarthy's life was his marriage on September 29, 1953, to Miss Jean Kerr, his long-time assistant and collaborator in his Washington office. Later Senator and Mrs. McCarthy were to adopt a daughter, Tierny Elyzabeth, to round out the family. By all accounts Joe McCarthy was a loving husband and father, and the marriage was a happy one.

But his new-found domestic bliss did not long delay the senator's goal of destroying the Menace. His next target, he hinted to reporters, would be the Army Signal Corps's laboratories and installation at Fort Monmouth, New Jersey. This center was devoted to high-level top-secret research of various kinds; evidence of espionage or subversion here would touch a very vital nerve. So delicate was the matter that Senator McCarthy decided to conduct his investigation not in Washington but in closed sessions at the U.S. Federal Courthouse on Foley Square, New York City. No one ever suggested that by moving into this historic building McCarthy may have been hoping to stir public memories of the trial and conviction of the leadership of the Communist Party which also had taken place there.

In any event the closed hearings opened on October 8, 1953. Scores of Fort Monmouth army and civilian employees were questioned. Headlines began blooming in the press about "sensational disclosures," "nests of spies," "many suspensions," etc. Because the hearings were closed to press and public, these headlines proceeded from information given out by McCarthy and Cohn. As to what was really happening behind closed doors in the Federal Courthouse, Harry Green, a conservative New Jersey lawyer who represented some of the Fort Monmouth employees being questioned, wrote a description that appeared in the *New Jersey Law Review*:

". . . You walk in with your client, into a room bustling with movement and excitement . . . you are placed before a long table with four or five inquisitors thereat . . .

"Counsel for the witness is immediately told off, as follows: 'You will be permitted to sit with your client; you may consult with each other, but you are not to participate in any other manner in the hearing. You are not to ask questions; you are not to cross-examine; you are not to make objections; you are not to argue. You may remain under these conditions.'

"Your client is then subjected to a hydra-headed interrogation from all around the table, and to say that he is confused is to put it mildly.

"You sit there like a wooden Indian, and you hear questions that seem incredible. Here is an inquisitorial example:

" 'I am troubled by what a witness testified to yesterday. I asked him if you (your client) were a Communist and he refused to answer upon the ground that it might incriminate him. Why should he refuse to answer? It seems to me from this that you are a Communist.' "

Had Attorney Green read of the experience of *New York Post* Editor James A. Wechsler just a few months previously before this same subcommittee (he had been haled before it because the *Post* had audaciously criticized Joe McCarthy), he would have been even more intrigued. For when Wechsler displayed copies of articles from various Communist journals denouncing him as proof that he was certainly not beloved by the Party, McCarthy in a brilliant leap of imagination demanded: "Did you write those statements?"

Momentarily stunned, Wechsler later wrote: "In what I will always recall as one of the most preposterous moments of my life, I thereupon solemnly denied under oath that I was the author of the Communist statement denouncing myself!"

The Fort Monmouth hearings dragged on. Many employees faced the inquisitors; many disbelieving and frustrated attorneys attempted to defend them. All denied charges of espionage, sabotage or subversion, but as usual these denials never overtook the headlines of McCarthy's charges. Some employees, like witnesses facing other congressional committees, on the advice of their attorneys refused to answer questions. They preferred to invoke the Fifth Amendment to the Constitution which stated that no American should be forced to incriminate himself. Of course McCarthy and Cohn immediately began shouting about "Fifth Amendment Communists." To avail oneself of one's constitutional rights was, to them, clear evidence of communism.

The Fifth Amendment, like most American constitutional concepts, had developed from the old Anglo-Saxon common law and had been specifically designed to operate in just these circumstances. If, for example, a witness refused to answer one of the permanent subcommittee's questions, he could be cited, tried and jailed for contempt of Congress. But these questions were designed to trap witnesses into incriminating themselves. Suppose you were the witness undergoing inquisition. One of the subcommittee staff asks you: "Have you ever been affiliated with any Communist organizations?" You *must* respond to the question. Unfortunately, you do not know all the many organizations considered to be Communist-affiliated by the U.S. attorney general. You do not know exactly what "affiliation with any Communist organizations" means. Does it mean that you were once a member? Does it mean you once, as a non-member, attended some function of such an organization? Does it mean that such an organization, without your knowledge, perhaps once used your name for some purpose? Does it mean that one or another member of your family or perhaps a friend was once associated with such an organization, and because you associate with this person you are indirectly associated with that organization also? Remember, your attorney cannot answer for you or intervene in the hearings on your behalf. He can only advise you regarding your answer. If you lie, of course you will be prosecuted for perjury. But, suppose you answer truthfully to the best of your knowledge that you have never been affiliated with any Communist organization. In that case *you still risk prosecution for perjury.*

How? Consider: you do not know who has brought charges against you; you do not know who the witnesses may be against you; you do not know what evidence has been presented against you; you do not even know what the specific charges against you are. Suppose your memory fails. Suppose you are confused by the many possibilities for error listed above. Suppose you are the victim of some neurotic or fanatic government informer. Have you confidence in these hysterical times that a jury will believe you rather than the government informer? You know very well that if the government informer perjures himself he will not be prosecuted —the government protects its informers. You know of many people who have been jailed through such action. You have heard of others who have been "framed" by government agents using forged evidence. At the very least you realize that your defense, in case of a perjury citation, is going to be very long, very complicated and extremely costly. Furthermore, while you are defending yourself, you and your family will be stigmatized as "reds" simply because of the publicity generated by the case. You will probably be suspended from your job, and then how will you pay for your defense?

Considering all these factors you follow your attorney's whispered advice and respond to the question: "I refuse to answer that question on the grounds that my answer may incriminate me." (And you offer up a silent blessing to the wisdom of the Founding Fathers who provided you and every other American with this refuge from the persecution of a powerful government.) You have used, as is your right, the Fifth Amendment to the United States Constitution. But *even so*, you will suffer. For it will be announced to the press that you have "taken the Fifth." And most Americans, perhaps including your employer, who understand very little about constitutional law and privileges will assume you have something to hide.

Even those Americans in a position to know or be informed about constitutional law will hound you. For example, Francis Cardinal Spellman, speaking to a Catholic audience on October 24, 1953: ". . . there are many individuals who have seriously compromised themselves by a flat refusal to state whether they are now or have been Communists. It is impossible for me to understand why any American should refuse to declare himself free of Communist affiliations, unless he has something to hide." In the next chapter we will consider the fate of some Americans who did *not* avail themselves of the Fifth Amendment.

Was there no other way? Columbia University professor of philosophy Corliss Lamont thought there might be. He appeared before McCarthy's permanent subcommittee on September 23, 1953. There was little doubt that Professor Lamont had long endorsed Soviet-American friendship, that he held political opinions considered "radical" by some Americans and that he might even be considered "sympathetic" to communism by people who made it their business to stigmatize the views of their fellow citizens. As for being a Communist, the professor testified: "To dispose of a question causing current apprehension, I am a loyal American and I am not now and never have been a member of the Communist Party." But beyond this statement Professor Lamont was not willing to go. He refused to answer subcommittee questions, not on the grounds of self-incrimination provided by the Fifth Amendment, but rather on the grounds clearly stated in the First Amendment to the Constitution: that no branch, committee, or member of the government had any right to pry into his private beliefs or opinions. He was not, after all, in government employ; he was a private citizen. His faith, his politics, and his thoughts were his private affair; they were none of the government's business. What happened next was highly instructive.

First of all, McCarthy recommended to the Senate that Lamont be cited for contempt of Congress on technical grounds. That august but quavering body duly brought in an indictment. The U.S. Department of Justice now took over the prosecution, and hearings were scheduled in New York Federal Court. Professor

Lamont's attorney argued that the indictment was illegal. His argument was not only based on grounds provided by the First Amendment, it was based also on the fact that the Permanent Subcommittee of the Committee on Government Operations had never been granted authority by Congress to conduct investigations on "subversive activities." One can almost hear the sigh of relief behind the verdict of the New York Federal Court, which, in deciding in Lamont's favor (on July 27, 1955), based its ruling on the illegality of the investigation, not on an affirmation of the First Amendment. "This disposition," declared the court, "makes it unnecessary to determine the constitutional and other issues so vigorously pressed for disposition by the defendants." The Justice Department (which consistently refused to prosecute its own perjured informers) was a veritable bulldog when it came to the prosecution of possible "reds." The department fought the case up to the Court of Appeals and a year later (on August 14, 1956) once again lost. In fact the court reprimanded the government attorneys for "attempting to hang onto and retain for trial indictments for offenses which cannot be supported in law." But again the Court of Appeals refused to rule on the vital question of Professor Lamont's rights under the First Amendment. Like the lower court, it dismissed the indictment on lesser grounds. Those were not the times for ringing affirmations of American rights under the United States Constitution. It is noteworthy that Professor Lamont's eventual victory was so costly in legal fees as to be far beyond the pockets of most Americans.

Of course, questions of constitutional law never troubled Tail-Gunner Joe. His aim was publicity, nothing more. The hearings on espionage and subversion at Fort Monmouth continued to drag scare headlines through the press, witnesses before the Grand Inquisition and red herrings across the American political scene. In the end, after exhaustive investigation not only by the permanent subcommittee but by the U.S. Army and the FBI as well, no spies or saboteurs were uncovered at Fort Monmouth, nor was there even one single "security risk."

None of this mattered. It did not matter that 1953 had seen Tail-Gunner Joe in full retreat on several occasions. The denunciation of the Protestant clergy did not matter; President Dwight D. Eisenhower's reproof did not matter; the dramatic departure of the Democratic members from the permanent subcommittee did not matter; the absurdity of the Cohn-Schine performance in Europe did not matter; the fiasco of the Fort Monmouth hearings did not matter. McCarthy's was by now a name with which to conjure. Political myth held that his legions were immense, his power fateful. His very name had become a new noun in the English language. For now when people sought to describe the entire spectrum of red-baiting, the total avocation of the Menace peddlers, they simply called it "McCarthyism." But they did so discreetly.

How discreetly was evidenced by the actions of the Senate during the opening weeks of 1954. At this time the Senate had to vote new funds to continue the work of the permanent subcommittee. By refusing funds, or cutting them to the bone, the Senate could effectively emasculate the subcommittee. But 1954 was a year of midterm congressional elections. Who under these circumstances would risk incurring the wrath of the man who had toppled Senators Tydings, Lucas, and Benton?

Preparing to appeal for new funds, McCarthy did make one concession. He informed Senators Jackson, Symington, and McClellan that hereafter they would have their proper say on the permanent subcommittee regarding the hiring and firing of its staff. Of course this was merely a maneuver; McCarthy had no intention of firing Roy Cohn or any other of his hand-picked red-baiters as the Democrats had demanded. Nevertheless, mollified by this formal surrender, the Democrats returned to the subcommittee. Soon a frightened Senate, by 85–1 vote, appropriated ample funds for McCarthy's continuing inquisition. The lone courageous dissenter was Arkansas Democratic Senator J. William Fulbright. This victory over the Senate on February 2, 1954, may represent McCarthy's greatest triumph. By that time every senator and every Washington politician had had ample opportunity to learn just what McCarthyism represented. The renewed funding of the subcommittee was a Senate vote of confidence in McCarthyism.

Yet this vote was McCarthy's last great victory, though none could know it at the time. But before we investigate the factors that combined to bring about the senator's downfall, let us examine some of the direct and indirect consequences of the malignancy named after him. For the effect of McCarthyism on the American body politic was more widespread and poisonous than even his enemies could have realized.

CHAPTER EIGHT

The Climate of Fear

What innocent person have I injured? I've asked that question lots of times—on forums and in speeches—and nobody ever tells me. I have never yet had anyone give me the name of a single innocent person who has been hurt by my methods.

—SEN. JOSEPH R. McCARTHY (R., WIS.)

To COMPREHEND the full impact of the specter men call "McCarthyism" on American life it is necessary first to understand that the engines of destruction associated with the ism were by no means limited to the various committees and subcommittees graced by the presence of the junior senator from Wisconsin. Long before the arrival of Tail-Gunner Joe, the United States government had devised machinery for the pursuit, snaring, and persecution of suspect citizens. In a sense, "McCarthyism" simply fueled this machinery, publicized its workings and distributed its "benefits" into areas of American life it otherwise might not have penetrated.

In the legislative branch, for example, apart from McCarthy's permanent subcommittee, there existed the venerable House Un-American Activities Committee. HUAC (as this granddaddy of all governmental witch-hunting committees was called) was no mean device for the entrapment of "pinks, punks and perverts," as McCarthy called its victims. On the other hand the Senate could boast its own Senate Internal Security Committee, headed, before 1952, by Nevada's Democratic Senator Patrick A. McCarran. It was to this distinguished representative of Nevada's mining and gambling interests that the nation owed the fearsome Internal

Security Act of 1950. By the terms of this piece of legislation a five-member Subversive Activities Control Board had been established with authority to examine American minds for traces of heresy. Furthermore, the act provided for the registration of American Communists and "other subversives" as "agents of a foreign power." And finally, this neo-Fascist addition to the body of American legislation provided for the construction of about half a dozen concentration camps (still in existence) for the incarceration of anyone deemed "subversive" in times of national emergency. After 1952, the Senate Internal Security Committee was headed by Indiana's Republican Senator William E. Jenner, a longtime McCarthy supporter and a stout defender of the republic against the dangers of free thought.

The executive branch of the government maintained a mighty arsenal for the destruction of its internal enemies. Aside from the various loyalty review boards established under President Truman (essentially defensive weapons), it could rely upon Treasury agents, the Secret Service, the Central Intelligence Agency, and of course the Federal Bureau of Investigation, headed by the redoubtable J. Edgar Hoover. Whatever the vicissitudes of political strife, even during times when the chief executive was *persona non grata* in the halls of Congress, these federal agencies could be counted on to cooperate eagerly with the legislative branch.

Thus many of the victims of McCarthyism were not, in fact, pursued to their doom by Joe McCarthy himself. It was often sufficient for Tail-Gunner Joe to simply mention names on the Senate floor while testifying before some committee. These persons immediately would be sucked into the tentacles of the government's apparatus, where their actual destruction would often be accomplished. This apparatus included not only the legislative committees hungering for evidence of perjury or contempt; not only the various police agencies adept at spying, intimidation and, on occasion, the fabrication of questionable "evidence"; not only the courts before which, in those days, a person tainted with accusations of "subversion" was often deemed guilty until proved innocent by a jury of his peers; it consisted also of that group of ex-Communist informers and *agents-provocateurs* which, as we have seen, included neurotics, psychotics and just plain ornery types eager to drag down into their personal hell any citizen offered to them by their government. These informers or, more often, accusers could point the finger of guilt at anyone, secure in the knowledge that they themselves would never face perjury charges.

How all this machinery meshed to snare the unwary was well illustrated in the case of Professor Owen J. Lattimore.

In a previous chapter we saw how in 1950 Professor Lattimore stoutly defended himself and as stoutly assailed Senator McCarthy before the Tydings committee. From these hearings Owen Lattimore emerged apparently triumphant. He might well have assumed that his name was cleared and that the cloud of suspicion had passed from him. But if so he reckoned without the determination and perseverance of his tormentors.

Owen Lattimore had been involved in the work of the Institute of Pacific Relations during the late 1930s. During that time he had edited the Institute's magazine *Pacific Affairs*. On February 7, 1951, agents of the Senate Internal Security Committee (along with McCarthy aide Don Surine) stole from the farm of Edward C. Carter (former secretary-general of IPR) outside Pittsfield, Massachusetts, several filing cabinets containing documents, copies of correspondence and memoranda relating to IPR affairs. This material had long before been examined by the FBI and found worthless. Of course the FBI had been looking for evidence, not publicity. The seizure of these files was hailed by McCarran and McCarthy as a decisive breakthrough in their battle against the Menace. Among the documents stolen were various memoranda and letters composed by Owen Lattimore. And if the FBI thought this material valueless, Joe McCarthy, still smarting from Lattimore's attack on him before the Tydings committee, was certain it would provide subversive evidence. In the hands of McCarran's Senate Internal Security Committee it certainly did. It provided evidence that Professor Lattimore's memory was not infallible (some of the dates he had given before the Tydings committee were a year or two off) and that his views in the late 1930s had leaned further toward the left than was fashionable in the 1950s.

One year later, in February 1952 (an election year), Owen Lattimore was once more summoned to Washington. There he was called before Senator McCarran's Internal Security Committee and confronted with the "new" evidence that had been distilled from the stolen IPR files. Still plucky, the professor attempted to read (as was his right) an opening statement to the assembled inquisitors. But it was immediately evident that this time Lattimore was to be caught. Senate usage, courtesy, and common decency were tossed aside by the committee members and their staff. So often was Lattimore interrupted during his "reading" of his opening statement that in three hours he had managed to get through exactly eight lines of it!

Lattimore's attorney protested against the interruptions and harassment to which his client was subjected—and was threatened with expulsion from the hearings. The *Washington Post* described the committee hearings:

"The subcommittee seems determined to beat Owen Lattimore into sheer physical exhaustion, to make fatigue and despair extort admissions which he would not make of his own free will. When Mr. Lattimore pleaded fatigue and asked for a respite the other day, Senator McCarran said the members of the subcommittee were tired too. The subcommittee, with half a dozen members and two staff lawyers, all acting as prosecutors, has been able to question this lone witness in relays. For nine days it has subjected him to an incessant drumfire of interrogation. . . . But it is a frightening spectacle . . . to see a committee of the United States Senate bully and torment a witness in this fashion—as though he were in an arena, at bay, providing sport for the public."

McCarran and his cohorts refused again and again to allow Lattimore time to think about his answers (indeed, he was once instructed to answer without thinking), to refresh his memory about events that had occurred decades before, to consult his attorney, to answer any questions, no matter how complex or vague, with anything but a simple "yes" or "no." It was perfectly evident that the committee was determined to force the witness to commit "perjury" out of pure confusion. Of course, in the hallowed tradition of such hearings, Lattimore was never permitted to know who the witnesses were against him, what "evidence" the committee held, or even what specific charges he was defending himself against. Under these circumstances the outcome was a foregone conclusion.

On July 2, 1952, Nevada's silver-haired gift to the United States Senate, Pat McCarran, rose to demand that Owen Lattimore be cited for perjury. The committee's report charged that Lattimore had lied to the committee on five separate counts. He had claimed that Outer Mongolia was independent until after World War II, though he knew it was Soviet controlled; he had denied knowing that a man named Chi Ch'ao-ting was a Communist; he had denied knowing that Frederick Vanderbilt Field was a Communist two years earlier than he admitted; he had said he did not know that an author of several articles in *Pacific Affairs* was a Communist; and he had given an inaccurate description of his relationship with a person who had written about the committee hearings.

It might be supposed that this set of charges could never be used in court. To have mistaken the status of Outer Mongolia? Not to have known that an obscure Chinese person was a Communist? To have inaccurately dated his knowledge about Frederick Vanderbilt Field by two years? Nonsense. Yet Pat McCarran hounded the Justice Department for months until, somewhat reluctantly (the Department was aware of the flimsiness of the charges), it brought forward an indictment that was duly returned by a grand jury on December 16, 1952. Needless to say, the indictment centered on the basic accusation that Lattimore had lied when he denied being a Communist sympathizer ("com-symp" in the jargon of the day). Note that he was not accused of being a Communist or an agent of any Communist apparatus. He was accused of something so vague as to be unprovable.

At least so thought Federal Judge Luther W. Youngdahl, who dismissed four of the perjury counts against Lattimore (including the central "Communist sympathizer" count), after exhaustive hearings, on May 3, 1953. The judge pointed out to government attorneys that the indictment was a clear violation of the First Amendment. The Justice Department, under continuing pressure from McCarran, sent Judge Youngdahl's decision to the Federal Court of Appeals. Here, once again, the department was chastized. By a vote of eight to one the appellate justices supported Judge Youngdahl.

Its legal head bloody but unbowed, the Justice Department now started all over again. It obtained a fresh indictment from a new grand jury on October 7, 1954, which attempted to substantiate the "Communist sympathizer" charge by citing instances in which Professor Lattimore's views had paralleled those of the Communist Party. This new indictment was dismissed by Judge Youngdahl on January 18, 1955. He pointed out, for the instruction of the government attorneys, that the indictment this time violated not only the First but also the Sixth Amendment to the United States Constitution. The Sixth Amendment specifies that in criminal trials the accused must be "informed of the nature and cause of the accusation" against him. So vague were the Justice Department charges that no one could really determine the nature and cause of the accusations against Professor Owen Lattimore. Eschewing the opportunity to have their knuckles once again rapped by the Court of Appeals, the Justice Department formally dropped all charges against Lattimore on June 28, 1955.

A happy ending for the professor? Consider the many thousands of dollars in legal fees he had to pay. Consider the many long years during which he had to live in suspense and mental anguish. Consider the fact that to many Americans his indictment alone seemed proof positive of his guilt. Consider the fact that even though innocent he had been made into such a controversial figure that never again could he hope for government employment. Consider the fact that to the timid academic community his name had become so tarnished that even a university career was now closed to him. Professor Lattimore, reflecting on this treatment from the nation he had served, eventually emigrated to England.

The government's machinery for the destruction of careers was supplemented most effectively by the power of an all but irresponsible national press. With a few honorable exceptions (the *St. Louis Post-Dispatch*, the *New York Post*, the *Washington Post* and the *New York Times* head a very small list of newspapers which did *not* exploit McCarthy's views), the American press never failed to headline the senator's charges and ignore the denials and rebuttals of his victims. A man facing such irresponsible nationwide smearing would often decline public legal defense simply because he despised both his opponent and the arena in which the combat was held. The case of career diplomat John Carter Vincent illustrated this fact at a very early stage of the McCarthy crusade.

Vincent, like Owen Lattimore, was an "old China hand." Unlike Lattimore, he had been directly and continuously employed by the State Department since 1924. His many years of residence in the Far East had qualified him to become director of far eastern affairs in the department by 1945. Subsequently he had been appointed American minister to Switzerland. He had long been known in the department as a cautious, conservative diplomat, with political views somewhat to the right of, say, Richard M. Nixon.

Senator McCarthy, in his testimony before the Tydings committee, had declared that Vincent was a member of the "Lattimore clique" in the State Department. Because McCarthy also stated that Lattimore was Russia's "top agent in the United States," the national press intimated that Vincent also must be a spy. Reading these headlines at his post in Switzerland, Vincent declared that he would be content to let the State Department answer them. This the department did to the best of its ability. After an exhaustive analysis of Vincent's previous service, it announced that it could find nothing that would "even remotely substantiate Senator McCarthy's charges."

But the national publicity generated by these charges had already seriously damaged Vincent's usefulness as a representative of his country abroad. Furthermore, it had disgusted Vincent himself. Unwilling to lower himself, as he saw it, to do battle with a man like Joseph R. McCarthy, his career ruined not so much by the senator as by the publicity from the press, Vincent returned to the United States and retired from the diplomatic service—much to the relief of a nervous State Department.

At the time of Vincent's ordeal in 1952, the State Department (still under the control of the Democratic Truman administration) at least attempted to defend its personnel. But by 1954, when President Dwight D. Eisenhower presided over the nation's destiny and the State Department was in the hands of John Foster Dulles, this was no longer true. By that time it was no longer necessary to generate a national furor in order to assassinate the character and career of a foreign service officer, as the case of John Paton Davies, Jr., proved.

Davies was another of the China experts so hated by Alfred Kohlberg's China Lobby. He had been an adviser to General

"Vinegar Joe" Stilwell in China during World War II. His sin was that he had warned of the imminent Communist triumph in China and had urged that the United States maintain some line of communication to Mao Tse-tung's regime with a view to driving a wedge into Sino-Russian cordiality. Aside from this Davies held very conservative views. In 1950 he even advocated a preventive war against the Soviet Union. How all of this could be construed as "pro-Communist" was far from clear. But by the time the Eisenhower administration had comfortably settled itself in Washington, logic and reality had long since fled the nation's capital.

In November 1953 Tail-Gunner Joe, zeroing in on his own Republican administration, demanded that John Paton Davies, Jr. (whom he described as belonging to the Lattimore group in the State Department), be fired as a "security risk." Secretary of State John Foster Dulles knew that Davies had been investigated eight different times by loyalty boards—and eight times cleared of all suspicion. But McCarthy's blast was sufficient to send Davies before a ninth loyalty board. This time, although the board declared Davies absolutely innocent of "any Communist affinity," it declared him *indiscreet* in his advocacy of his ideas. Dulles asked Davies to resign, but Davies refused. Finally summoning the courage to commit the injustice demanded by McCarthy, John Foster Dulles fired Davies on November 4, 1954. What effect the Lattimore, Vincent, and Davies cases had on the State Depatment and on American foreign policy will be examined in a later chapter. For the moment it is interesting to note that Davies had to wait fifteen years for vindication. So lasting was the fear instilled into the Washington bureaucracy by Joe McCarthy that neither President John F. Kennedy nor President Lyndon B. Johnson (for most of his term) could muster sufficient courage to correct the wrong done to John Paton Davies, Jr. Not until January 1969 (with the Johnson administration leaving office in a matter of days) was the ex-foreign service officer publicly exonerated by being given a security clearance.

These cases and the many others to which McCarthy, McCarran, and several others devoted themselves were enacted upon the national stage with appropriate publicity and the intervention of highly placed public officials. Whereas all this was exceedingly damaging to the nation's government, the effects were by no means limited to Washington. The government's security machinery operated on every level of American life, and its victims were typical obscure Americans who underwent their crucifixion without benefit of an audience. It must be remembered that *anyone employed by any corporation or firm engaged in government-contracted work involving the use of "classified" materials or plans required a security clearance.* Thus local loyalty boards throughout the nation investigated the purity of thousands of ordinary citizens. And when these boards saw their superiors in Washington as well as congressmen, cabinet secretaries and presidents caving in before the winds of hate generated by Joe McCarthy, they went to ludicrous and sometimes vicious lengths to prove themselves equally zealous. In 1955 the Ford Foundation published a wide survey of the work of these local boards entitled: *Case Studies in Personnel Security,* from which the following instructive examples are drawn.

Take the case of Mr. X, a plumber residing and working on the West Coast. The contractor who employed him in a supervisory capacity received a government contract to do the plumbing for a West Coast air force base. The plans for this plumbing were "classified" materials, requiring a security check on all personnel handling them. The air force loyalty board decided that Mr. X. was a "bad security risk." Hence Mr. X could neither see nor handle the secret plumbing plans, nor could he work on the air force base project. Suddenly, without explanation, Mr. X was out of a job.

Bewildered, Mr. X made the rounds of local officialdom, from the nearest FBI office to the air force base security office. No one seemed to know anything about his plight. Finally he wrote to his congressman, who in turn asked the air force security board for an explanation. The "explanation" came through in September 1953—*more than one year after Mr. X had been fired.* The board informed Mr. X: "You are currently maintaining a close continuing association with your wife . . . who is stated to be engaged in activities of an organization which is Communist." Which organization? "The organization referred to," replied the board, "is the Communist Party."

Stunned and disbelieving, both Mr. X and his wife submitted affidavits declaring their innocence. Neither of them had ever been members of the Communist Party, nor had they ever received Communist literature into their home; they had never even discussed "Communist ideas." On the other hand, Mr. X's wife had told FBI investigators during their routine "clearance" of the plumber that her name had once been used without her permission or knowledge on a letterhead of the Spanish Anti-Fascist Refugee Committee (circa 1938), an organization later branded "subversive" by the U.S. attorney general. And, she told the FBI agents, once, while slightly tipsy at a cocktail party in Los Angeles in 1946, she made a five-dollar contribution to someone professing to represent some worthy cause the nature of which she could not recall but which was certainly *not* the Communist Party. On the subject of belonging to organizations, Mr. X's wife was very clear. She had been a member of the Newspaper Guild, the Business and Professional Women's Club, and the Campfire Girls.

At a hearing before the Appeals Division of the Western Industrial Security Board, Mr. and Mrs. X admitted to subscribing to their local daily newspaper, *Breeders' Stock Magazine*, *Popular Mechanics*, *Ladies Home Journal* and *Cosmopolitan*. After thus establishing the purity of their reading matter, Mr. and Mrs. X also deposed that they never discussed Mr. X's plumbing work at home. Finally the board admitted that there was nothing subversive about Mr. and Mrs. X. Thus Mr. X could receive clearance to handle classified plans.

Unfortunately this clearance could now do Mr. X no good. Nearly two years had passed since he had been fired. His former employer would not rehire him, nor was he to be reimbursed for the many months he had spent doing odd jobs or for the legal fees he faced. In effect his career had been ruined.

Consider the case of Mr. Y, a ship's butcher in the merchant marine. Mr. Y had gone to sea as a butcher since 1945, but in 1952 the coast guard declared him a security risk. Of course he was immediately fired from his job. It would never do to have subversive butchers lurking about American ports. But was Mr. Y subversive? No, he was not, declared the coast guard's security board. But "he has brothers who, according to this file, are believed to be affiliated with and associated with the Communist Party." What did Mr. Y know about his brothers' political beliefs? It turned out that Mr. Y knew nothing about such matters. All he knew, he stated, was that "outside of union activities . . . I haven't done nothing." This was considered uncooperative of Mr. Y. His condemnation was upheld and he was permanently "beached."

Sample questions asked by loyalty board officials in other cases:

"Don't you think that any person is a security risk who at one time or another associated with a Communist even though it was not a sympathetic association and even though the association terminated years ago?"

"Do you belong to the Book Find Club?"

"Don't you agree that there might be people with Communist tendencies in churches, whether or not such persons were actual party members?"

"Were you a regular purchaser of the *New York Times?*"

"Do you think that people testifying before congressional committees ought to hide behind the Fifth Amendment?"

"Are you going to cooperate with your government?"

It has been estimated that questions such as these were asked of about ten million Americans, divided into roughly equal parts among those employed by the government, those in the armed forces and those employed in government-contracted industry. This was intimidation on a truly vast scale. And even those Americans granted security clearance or those whose loyalty, after investigation, remained unquestioned were intimidated by the mere fact of investigation. The FBI or other security agents not only looked up the records in each individual case, they also made a practice of questioning relatives, friends, and ex-employers of those under examination. In short, the witch hunt was brought home to a substantial percentage of the citizenry in a very direct manner.

Also brought home to them was the flight from law and constitutional rights indulged in throughout the loyalty and security programs. When facing one of these boards, the person accused was presumed guilty until he could prove his innocence. But this was extremely difficult, because usually he was not informed as to the specific charges against him; he was not permitted to face or question his accusers, and he was denied access to the secret government file on which charges had been based. Furthermore, in a stunning reversal of common sense and common law, a person accused had to prove himself innocent *beyond a reasonable doubt.* If any doubt of his innocence prevailed in the mind of any of his inquisitors, the benefit of it was given to the government. To be sure, there were legal remedies against this preposterous procedure. An accused *could* appeal a verdict beyond the loyalty and security systems into the courts. But in every case where this was done, the government proved itself a master of delay, obfuscation and determination. Anyone proceeding to court against board rulings had to be prepared to wait years, to fight his way through every level up to and including the Supreme Court, and to pay for the litigation out of his own pocket. Ship's butchers and plumbers could not afford this procedure.

The atmosphere of dread and suspicion created by all this spread into areas far removed from the government machinery. Large corporations, fearful of their "image" before an apparently hysterical public, would often undertake, with the aid of private investigative agencies, inquiries of their own regarding their personnel. The policy behind this was to weed out anyone in any way "suspect" *before* such a person became officially enmeshed in the government machine, thereby hopefully avoiding the bad publicity associated with security check. Industries such as motion pictures, radio and television, especially sensitive to public goodwill, did not even bother employing private investigators. It was often sufficient for someone working in these fields merely to be mentioned on the various private blacklists circulated by lunatic-fringe extremists for that individual to suddenly become unemployable.

For example, take the case of radio actress Madeline Lee, who made a career out of gurgling like a baby over the airwaves. Accused of having been associated with a Communist-front organization years before, Miss Lee in 1953 was blacklisted; she could find no further employment on radio. Also defamed and blacklisted as a result of Madeline Lee's downfall were three other actresses who were not even accused of any political activity whatsoever. One lost her job because she bore the same name as Miss Lee; another because she happened to resemble Miss Lee; and the third because, although she neither resembled Miss Lee nor bore the same patronymic, she was unfortunate enough also to earn her living by squealing like a baby for radio audiences!

Especially vulnerable to smear and blacklisting were teachers and university professors. These were, after all, people who dealt with ideas at a time when all ideas were suspect. In this connection it must be recalled that many of the nation's largest universities are state universities directly dependent on state-appropriated funds for their operation. Thus the state often felt it had the duty to investigate the purity of those whom it indirectly salaried. As has been observed before, there were parallel state un-American activities committees in many sections of the country. Their intellectual and moral level was lower even than that prevailing in the House Un-American Activities Committee on which they modeled themselves. Professors appearing before any of these state committees were well advised to make use of the Fifth Amendment to protect themselves against perjured information and faked evidence. Yet recourse to this constitutional right was in itself generally sufficient to ruin an academic career. College presidents, dependent on state funds, could rarely summon the courage to incur the anger of state investigative committees. With the example of their unfortunate blacklisted colleagues before them, those teachers and professors as yet untouched sought to protect themselves by simply refusing to discuss any "controversial" ideas whatsoever, either among themselves or in their classrooms. After all, one never knew who might whisper into the ear of a heresy hunter. Student William F. Buckley, Jr. (who then, as now, had a fine nose for the intellectual "main chance"), published a book soon after his graduation entitled *God and Man at Yale* in which he did not hesitate to accuse individual professors, departments, and finally the university itself of inculcating the "spirit of materialism" (for this read "communism") into the student body.

So the universities fell silent during the 1950s and produced that strange phenomenon known as "the silent generation"—graduates who were afraid to speak out on any public issue whatsoever, who sought refuge in the anonymity of corporate employment, and who above all devoted their talents to a search for security and conformity.

It must be pointed out, however, that in this respect university students of the fifties differed but little from their fellow Americans. Attempting to sample the atmosphere of fear generated by the triumph of the Menace peddlers, various newspapers from time to time in different parts of the country sent forth reporters bearing "petitions" or questionnaires to test public reaction. Typical of the results were those harvested by the Madison (Wisconsin) *Capital-Times*. In midsummer 1951 this newspaper composed a "petition" made up verbatim of quotes taken from the Declaration of Independence and the Constitution of the United States. Reporters asked citizens if they would sign this petition. Ninety-nine percent of those asked refused. Some declared that the sentiments expressed therein were obviously subversive, but most would give no reason for not signing. Clearly this "silent majority" was fearful of even discussing the matter.

As pointed out earlier, not all of the national hysteria of the times can be ascribed to the activities of Joseph R. McCarthy. The government machinery existed before he enlisted in the crusade against the Menace. And although he gladly fed it victims, they were comparatively few in number. McCarthy's contribution to the panic that seized the American imagination during the 1950s was threefold. First, there was his cunning ability to generate headlines —and this kept the Menace in the forefront of the news day and night for several years. Secondly, there was the indisputable fact that the most powerful legislative and executive bodies in the country, as well as the men who presided over them, quailed in craven fear before Tail-Gunner Joe. And if the mighty cringed, what was the average man expected to do? Finally, McCarthy's success emboldened the many thousands of McCarthyite "minds" throughout the country to adopt his tactics in their own arenas. After all, if the senator could make a brilliant political career out of bullying, slander and recklessness, why not others?

But McCarthy, in the quote opening this chapter, declared that he had never injured a single innocent person by his methods. Of course the loophole in that statement was in the word "innocent." The senator would stoutly maintain that anyone chewed up in the governmental heresy machinery through his (McCarthy's) efforts could not be innocent. As we have seen, even such a moral authority as Francis Cardinal Spellman shared this opinion. Yet in at least one case, McCarthy's activities produced the ultimate dreadful response.

Mr. Raymond Kaplan was an engineer employed by the Voice of America. He had done much of the technical research that lay behind the decision on the geographical location of the Baker East and West transmitters. As McCarthy's assault on the Voice of America gained momentum, with newspapers screaming daily about Communist "sabotage" of the transmitters, Raymond Kaplan grew more and more depressed. He himself had not yet been accused of anything—indeed, afterwards, Senator McCarthy was to announce that he had never had any evidence of "wrongdoing of any kind" against Mr. Kaplan. Nonetheless, the fear generated by the McCarthy probe of the Baker East and West projects finally drove Raymond Kaplan to despair. He committed suicide by throwing himself under a truck in Boston. In letters left for his wife and children, Raymond Kaplan left no doubt as to why he had taken his life. He was, he feared, going to be made the ultimate victim in the VOA investigation although he was guilty of nothing. And in lines that went to the heart of the climate of fear gripping the nation, he wrote: "You see, once the dogs are set upon you, everything you have done from the beginning of time is suspect."

CHAPTER NINE

The Senator, the Private, and
the U.S. Army

> And why . . . have the demagogues triumphed so often?
> The answer is inescapable: because a group of political
> plungers has persuaded the President that McCarthyism
> is the best Republican formula for political success.
>
> —ADLAI STEVENSON

FRESH FROM the headlines of his Fort Monmouth investigation, with
the Democratic senators back on his permanent subcommittee and
with a juicy new appropriation all but unanimously voted him by
Congress, Senator McCarthy struck off on a new trail. It was a path
on which defeat awaited him in the end—but one he felt compelled
to travel for personal as well as public reasons.

The road began at Camp Kilmer, New Jersey, where, after their
usual sloppy "investigation," McCarthy and Roy Cohn discovered
a U.S. Army officer who was apparently a Communist. The officer's
name was Irving Peress and he was a dentist. Inducted into the
service in October 1952, Peress, in filling out his various army
forms, had invoked the Fifth Amendment when refusing to provide
information about his political beliefs. This fact had been overlooked by clerks in the Pentagon, and as was normal, Irving Peress
was commissioned a captain upon induction. The clerks' oversight
was not brought to Pentagon attention until February 1953. The
army thereupon investigated Captain Peress and in July 1953
recommended that he be separated from the service. But the mills
of the Pentagon grind slowly, and before they had thoroughly

separated wheat from chaff in the Peress case, Captain Peress, along with 7,000 other army doctors and dentists, had been promoted to major—as was required by his length of service. This promotion of the "Fifth Amendment dentist" had gone through in October 1953. By December of that same year the army had definitely decided to rid itself of the suspect dentist. The question was: How? To give Major Peress a dishonorable discharge would require court-martial proceedings. Besides, the major had committed no crime. He had not perjured himself. All along he had kept well within his constitutional rights under the Fifth Amendment. And he had been a good soldier in all other respects. The only alternative was to give the major a normal honorable discharge; this the army decided to do.

Unfortunately for everyone concerned, Senator McCarthy learned about the Peress matter before the major's discharge could go through. On January 30, 1954, Peress was summoned before McCarthy's permanent subcommittee. There he again invoked the Fifth Amendment. The next day he applied for immediate discharge; and on February 2 he received it, despite McCarthy's urgent demand that the army hold the dentist for court-martial. Peress, it appeared, had won his race against time—but the army had not. "Who promoted Peress?" roared McCarthy—and the hunt was on!

By Thursday, February 18, McCarthy's hunt had turned up Brigadier General Ralph W. Zwicker, commandant of Camp Kilmer. General Zwicker was a bemedaled hero of World War II who of course had nothing directly to do with the Peress matter; he had merely followed superior orders when he issued Peress his discharge. Nonetheless, on February 18 he found himself facing McCarthy and Roy Cohn at a closed hearing in New York. In his usual fashion McCarthy propounded to General Zwicker a set of hypothetical questions which bore almost no relationship to the real facts in the case.

It was useless for General Zwicker to explain that he had no more authority to either discharge or retain Major Peress in the service than he had to promote him. "Don't give me that double-talk!" McCarthy snapped. ". . . I cannot understand you sitting there, general, a general in the army, and telling me that you could not, would not, hold up his discharge. . . ."

Should a general who had acted as Zwicker had in the Peress affair be kept in his country's service? McCarthy demanded. General Zwicker protested; the matter was not for a hypothetical general to decide. That decision belonged to higher army authority.

"You are ordered to answer, general . . . You will answer that question unless you take the Fifth Amendment. I do not care how long we stay here. You are going to answer it."

"Do you mean how I feel about Communists?" the by now thoroughly confused general asked.

"I mean exactly what I asked you," thundered McCarthy, "nothing else. And anyone with the brains of a five-year-old child can understand that question. . . ."

General Zwicker eventually declared that a hypothetical general, provided he was acting under competent orders, should not be discharged.

"Then, general," McCarthy roared righteously, "you should be removed from any command. Any man who has been given the honor of being promoted to general and who says, 'I will protect another general who protected Communists,' is not fit to wear that uniform, general. I think it is a tremendous disgrace to the army. . . . You will be back here, general." And so McCarthy dismissed a man who wore the Silver Star, the Legion of Merit, the Legion of Honor and the Croix de Guerre among his many decorations for service to his country.

This unwarranted humiliation of a field-grade officer was too much for Secretary of the Army Robert T. Stevens to swallow. Obtaining an affidavit from General Zwicker as to how he had been treated by McCarthy, Stevens called a press conference. He declared that he had ordered General Zwicker to make no further appearances before McCarthy's permanent subcommittee. "I cannot permit loyal officers of our armed forces to be subjected to such unwarranted treatment. The prestige and morale of our armed forces are too important to the security of the nation to have them weakened by unfair attacks upon our officer corps," he said.

Not deigning to reply to this, McCarthy let Roy Cohn speak for him. The Peress case, Cohn said, represented "stupidity at best, and treason at worst. Those who committed it are now being shielded by order of the secretary of the army." Stevens himself would be called before the permanent subcommittee, Cohn hinted ominously.

Horrified by the looming clash between a Republican secretary of the army and a Republican senator, various politicians now rushed forward to make peace between them. Chief among these was Vice-President Richard M. Nixon—a man who had himself used many of McCarthy's tactics with great success, who was an outspoken admirer of the junior senator from Wisconsin, and who had served as unofficial go-between from the Eisenhower White House to Tail-Gunner Joe. At Nixon's urging, Senator McCarthy and Secretary Stevens lunched together on February 24, 1954. The army secretary emerged from this love feast (the menu featured fried chicken) under the impression that he had won his point: army officers would never again be given the "Zwicker treatment" by McCarthy. Unfortunately, this was not the way McCarthy recalled the luncheon conversation. He told the press that Stevens had given way all along the line. Soon newspaper headlines bloomed about Stevens's "retreat," about his "surrender" to the senator. Even the *Times* of London was moved to comment: "Senator McCarthy achieved today what General Burgoyne and General Cornwallis never achieved—the surrender of the American Army." Pentagon morale plunged as sharply as State Department morale had plunged earlier. Stevens himself, aghast at the damage done by his luncheon with McCarthy, tearfully informed aides that he would now have to resign.

But this final capitulation to Tail-Gunner Joe was something that the Republican administration could not countenance. It would destroy morale throughout the armed services, split the Republican Party (Stevens was, after all, a *Republican* cabinet member) and tarnish the good name of President (ex-General of The Armies) Dwight David Eisenhower. The occupant of the White House, who for so long had ignored McCarthy and McCarthyism on the theory that if he didn't look it would all somehow go away, now was forced to act. At the suggestion of several Eisenhower aides, Stevens issued his own statement to the press. In it he simply refuted McCarthy. He had never retreated from principle, he said; he would continue to protect army officers from harassment. In effect, Stevens was saying McCarthy had lied. Eisenhower's press secretary hastened to assure assembled reporters that the president backed Stevens's statement "one hundred percent." At long last McCarthy was challenged by the top leadership of his own party—by one of the most politically popular presidents in American history. The question that most intrigued observers was: How could McCarthy ever have allowed himself to fall into this position? Why had he ever taken on that most assuredly patriotic organization, the U.S. Army? The answer to this question was both ridiculous and bizarre.

When G. David Schine was about to be drafted into the United States Army, horror seems to have been aroused in Roy Cohn's patriotic breast. For several weeks he nagged at generals, at assistant secretaries, and at Secretary of the Army Stevens himself seeking to have Schine exempted from military service. When it became evident that this would not occur, Cohn turned all his immense energies toward trying to get a commission for his friend. But no one could be found to advocate that G. David Schine be granted a commission, although the matter was given consideration by top Pentagon officials. Finally, on November 3, 1954, the dreadful event occurred: G. David Schine was drafted into the army as a private. He was sent to Fort Dix, New Jersey, for his basic training.

But Private Schine's army was not the same as other enlisted men's army. While other trainees might receive one or two passes during their four weeks of basic training, Private Schine received no less than sixteen. While his less fortunate comrades performed close-order drill, Private Schine was excused so that he could place 250 long-distance telephone calls. Though other soldiers might walk in awe of their company commander, Private Schine was in the habit of throwing his arm around the captain's shoulder and explaining how he intended to "modernize the army." And whereas other soldiers suffered the indignities of KP in mute acceptance of their fate, Private Schine would call Mr. Roy Cohn, who in turn would call General Zwicker or the Pentagon or Secretary of the Army Stevens to make sure his favorite draftee did not have to peel potatoes. Indeed, the army career of Private G. David Schine was an enlisted man's dream, and it had all the elements of low farce. But that was only one side of the matter.

To protect the interests of his friend, Roy Cohn did not simply appeal—he threatened. He threatened Secretary Stevens with all sorts of investigations (of which Fort Monmouth was the opener) and the detonation of every sort of scandal (of which the Peress case would serve as an example) unless Stevens and the army treated his buddy "right." In monitored telephone calls Cohn subjected Stevens and other officials to the most abusive and obscene language in his bullying campaign. In sum, Roy Cohn was attempting to blackmail the United States Army.

What was McCarthy's stake in all this? He had hinted to Secretary Stevens months earlier that he couldn't care less how Private G. David Schine was treated. In fact, it was apparent that the senator considered the playboy a nuisance. But he backed up Roy Cohn in everything he did on Schine's behalf. Observers were led to believe that Cohn had some sort of "hold" on McCarthy, but what could it be? Also, why was Roy Cohn so hysterical over the rather normal experiences of his friend G. David Schine in the army? What was at the root of so passionate an attachment? And again, what was the nature of Cohn's relationship with Tail-Gunner Joe? These were questions which discreet observers never asked. Yet aside from immediate personal considerations, there remained a deeper question demanding exploration: why did Joseph R. McCarthy hate the United States Army?

That he did so can hardly be denied. His career of national notoriety started with an attack on the army when he injected himself into the Malmedy massacre hearings. On that occasion he accused the army of cruelty, double-dealing, the torture of prisoners and unconscionable prevarication. Now he was about to close his career with a renewed assault on the army, during which he would accuse it of high treason. The implicit irony of the fact that super-patriot Joe McCarthy both opened and concluded his career by viciously assailing that most super-patriotic organization has not been lost upon historians. But there is more than irony here. During both investigations McCarthy displayed more than his usual brutality, more than his normal spleen. In his abusive and contemptuous handling of army officer witnesses he showed what can only be described as a deep personal detestation of the army and all its members and functions. Why? Was that not a strange role for a super-patriot to play?

There was nothing in McCarthy's wartime experience (he served in the United States Marine Corps) that might have ignited a hatred of the army; nor can any specific personal factor in his childhood or career be uncovered to account for it. Yet there was a nonspecific factor. Joe McCarthy was a product of the traditionally rural, populist Midwest in which the so-called eastern establishment (intellectuals, politicians, diplomats, financiers—the suave, sophisticated manipulators of national power) was both hated and feared. It is quite possible that McCarthy unconsciously associated America's top military leadership with this detestably "superior" establishment. It would not matter that such military leadership was drawn from every state, class and condition in the nation; they were all graduates of that snobbish eastern academy, West Point, weren't they? Did not the generals and admirals display that same smugly confident, superciliously condescending image that was the everlasting face of the establishment? Did they not, like their colleagues in the State Department, look down on and despise the uncouth, untutored, unsophisticated farm boy from Wisconsin?

People are almost always prisoners of their own myths—and Joe McCarthy was no exception. The myth of the all-powerful, sneeringly superior eastern establishment was, in a way, bred into McCarthy's bones. If this affords some explanation of his attitude toward the United States Army, it may also shed some light on his basic attitude toward the entire governing structure he so savagely attacked. Believing as he did that cultured people in all walks of life, in all branches of government *must* despise him, McCarthy had long since determined *to make those who despised him fear him.* In this he was, for a long time, successful. But his efforts of course only assured him of a real and increasing loathesomeness from those he attacked. Thus, like so many neurotics, McCarthy subconsciously endeavored to establish the reality of his worst fears. In effect he was saying to himself: "I know you all hate and despise me—and I'll prove it by making you hate and despise me." And so, both in McCarthy's fantasy and in the real world, the time bomb of his feud with the United States Army ticked away. . . .

Meanwhile, a private American citizen who had followed the

career of the junior senator from Wisconsin since its inception decided that he could stomach no more. He was Edward R. Murrow, a world-famous foreign correspondent during World War II who now conducted his own television program entitled *See It Now*. Murrow had faced German bombs during the blitz against England, and his shortwave broadcasts to America ("This is London . . .") had been classics of their kind. Ed Murrow was a man passionately attached to those American ideals incorporated in such documents as the Declaration of Independence and the Constitution of the United States. He had watched in mounting horror and revulsion as Joe McCarthy trampled on them. Now he decided to act. On March 9, 1954, Ed Murrow devoted the entire *See It Now* telecast to a vivisection of Senator Joseph R. McCarthy.

Made up of miles of film showing McCarthy in action, Murrow's show was devastating. He made but little comment, interjecting only when necessary to point out the senator's lies. Instead he let Senator McCarthy expose Senator McCarthy. And there it was—the browbeating of witnesses, the bullying, the arrogant sneer forever plastered on McCarthy's heavy face, the ranting, nagging voice rich in the tones of paranoia and hate, the shiftiness, the basic cowardice—the bare skeleton of McCarthy's character was laid open by one of the most skillfully wielded scalpels in the television industry. As the program ended, Murrow permitted himself a personal statement. "We must not confuse dissent with disloyalty," Murrow told his audience. "We will not walk in fear, one of another. We will not be driven by fear into an age of unreason if we dig deep in our history and doctrine, and remember that we are not descended from fearful men. . . ."

At no small risk to his career, Edward R. Murrow did what so many other more highly placed Americans should long since have done: he recalled his fellow citizens to reason and decency. The response was overwhelming. From all over the country mail poured into CBS, and it was highly favorable to Murrow and highly critical of McCarthy. Evidently political and personal morality had not been completely extinguished as yet in the United States.

Then, on March 11, 1954, the McCarthy-Cohn-Army time bomb exploded with a roar that shocked the nation. Secretary of the Army Stevens released a detailed report on the ways in which

Radio and television newscaster Edward R. Murrow required just thirty minutes on his CBS program See It Now *to shoot* Tail-Gunner Joe *down in flames before the American people.*

McCarthy and Cohn had attempted to blackmail the army into granting preferential treatment to G. David Schine. The report was studded with transcripts of conversations (with Cohn's obscenities excised); it was specific in its details. Americans who had never seemed to mind Senator McCarthy's assaults on their rights and liberties or his persecutions of their fellow citizens were shocked. Too many millions of them had themselves served in their nation's armed forces; too many of them mourned loved ones killed on battlefields ranging from Germany to Guadalcanal to Korea. This shabby attempt to protect an ex-playboy from the mild rigors of army basic training outraged something deep within the national psyche.

Naturally, McCarthy did not take this report lying down. In his best tradition he countered with accusations of his own. Oh, yes, there had been blackmail, all right. But it had been the other way around. The army, by its treatment of Private Schine (a "hostage," according to McCarthy), had been attempting to blackmail McCarthy and the permanent subcommittee into calling off their investigations of "communism in the armed forces."

And with that counter-blast from Tail-Gunner Joe, confrontation could no longer be avoided. Either a United States senator or the United States Army had lied to the American people and to Congress. Much as Republicans (and many Democrats) would have been glad to forget the whole affair, this simply could not be done. Even McCarthy's warmest Senate supporters, sniffing the political air, conceded that this matter would have to be thrashed out fully and publicly.

Ironically, the Senate committee that would have to investigate was none other than McCarthy's permanent subcommittee. Because he was himself a principal in the affair, McCarthy temporarily left both his seat (which was filled by Republican Senator Henry Dworshak of Idaho) and his chairmanship of the subcommittee, which then passed to a very unhappy Senator Karl Mundt. The permanent subcommittee hired Tennessee lawyer Ray H. Jenkins as counsel. He was a tall, rangy, aggressive attorney famed for never having lost a client to the executioner. The army retained Boston attorney Joseph Nye Welch of the respected firm of Hale & Dorr, who declined to accept payment of any kind for his services.

Committee Counsel Ray Jenkins (sporting the rose) admonishes McCarthy against abusive language during the Army-McCarthy hearings. Roy Cohn listens glumly.

Welch's conservative dress, fatherly appearance (he was sixty-three), impeccable manners and gentle voice disguised a razor-sharp mind and a slyly sardonic wit.

The Army-McCarthy show (as the hearings were soon to be known to millions of Americans) was held in the ornate old Senate Caucus Room. Here klieg lights and television cameras were set up and scores of reporters, spectators and witnesses accommodated. It was later estimated that some fifty million Americans watched the hearings on their television sets—and the drama rarely flagged.

There was Ray Jenkins as committee counsel, but sometimes seeming to serve as McCarthy's personal attorney; there was Army Secretary Stevens, pale and haggard through days of intensive questioning and cross-examination; there was McCarthy, leaping up every other minute to cry, "A point of order! Mr. Chairman, may I raise a point of order?"; there was attorney Welch, quietly pinning one witness after another to the wall in his gentle manner;

and there were Roy Cohn, Don Surine, G. David Schine and all the other unsavory characters from McCarthy's stable. The hearings were a clash of wills, a contest of personalities, a dogged search for the truth through thickets of verbiage. For weeks the nation watched in fascination as Joseph Welch exposed McCarthy and Cohn as liars and cheats.

There was, for example, the celebrated case of the cropped photo (shades of the campaign against Millard Tydings!). This was a picture presented to the subcommittee by attorney Jenkins, showing Secretary Stevens standing alone with Private Schine at Maguire Air Force Base near Fort Dix. This, hinted Jenkins, proved that Stevens was trying to be especially nice and considerate to Private Schine by agreeing to pose alone with him, thus hoping to influence McCarthy into calling off his investigative hounds. But the next day Joseph Welch produced an enlargement of the same photo. It showed Stevens and Schine and also Air Force Colonel Jack T. Bradley, as well as the sleeve of a fourth individual. The picture presented by Jenkins had been purposely cropped in an attempt to deceive the subcommittee. Of course, Welch explained gently, he was certain that Jenkins had no part in this attempted fraud. But who had committed it? A long procession of McCarthy agents now took the stand, and each claimed he had had no part in the matter. Memories collapsed right and left as McCarthy's men abandoned ship; no one, it seemed, was responsible for the fraudulent photo. At last attorney Welch narrowed the field down to McCarthy agent James N. Juliana, a former FBI agent. The testimony:

WELCH: I find myself so puzzled to know why you just did not take a photostat of the picture that was delivered to you that afternoon and hand it over to Mr. Jenkins. Would you tell us how come you did not do this?

JULIANA: I just mentioned or just stated that I was under instructions to furnish a picture of only the two individuals.

WELCH: And who gave you these instructions?

JULIANA: Jenkins and—or Cohn.

. . . .

WELCH: Did you think this came from a pixie? Where did you think that this picture I hold in my hand came from?

Now how in the world did this happen? Joe McCarthy puzzles over the "doctored" photo of Private G. David Schine and Army Secretary Stevens which was introduced into the Army-McCarthy hearings by McCarthy's own staff.

JULIANA: I had no idea.

McCARTHY: (*interrupting*) Will counsel for my benefit define—I think he might be an expert on it—what a pixie is?

WELCH: Yes. I should say, Mr. Senator, that a pixie is a close relative of a fairy. Shall I proceed, sir? Have I enlightened you?

While the spectators laughed, Joe McCarthy and Roy Cohn glowered.

McCarthy's role as a self-proclaimed seditionist was made very clear through Welch's skillful cross-examination of the senator. For years Tail-Gunner Joe had urged public servants to turn over to him incriminating documents, whether such documents were classified as secret or not. The entire matter was brought out in regard to a letter written by FBI chief J. Edgar Hoover to G-2 (Army Intelligence). This classified letter had been stolen by someone and passed on to Joe McCarthy. Lawyer Welch attempted to find out from whom McCarthy had received the stolen document, but the senator consistently refused to answer, despite his solemn oath:

WELCH: Senator McCarthy, when you took the stand you knew of course that you were going to be asked about the letter, did you not?

McCARTHY: I assumed that would be the subject.

WELCH: And you of course understood that you were going to be asked the source from which you got it?

McCARTHY: . . . I won't answer that . . .

WELCH: Could I have the oath that you took read to us wholly by the reporter?

MUNDT: Mr. Welch, that doesn't seem to be an appropriate question . . . it's the same oath you took.

WELCH: The oath included a promise, a solemn promise by you to tell the truth and nothing but the truth. Is that correct, sir?

McCARTHY: Mr. Welch, you are not the first individual that tried to get me to . . . give out the names of my informants.

WELCH: I am only asking, sir, did you realize when you took the oath that you were making a solemn promise to tell the truth to this committee?

McCARTHY: I understand the oath, Mr. Welch.

WELCH: And when you took it, did you have some mental reservation, some Fifth or Sixth Amendment notion that you could measure what you would tell?

McCARTHY: I don't take the Fifth Amendment.

WELCH: Have you some private reservation when you take the oath . . . that lets you be the judge of what you will testify to?

McCARTHY: The answer is that there is no reservation about telling the whole truth.

WELCH: Thank you, sir. Then tell us who delivered the document to you?

McCARTHY: The answer is no. You will not get the information.

To this self-portrait of McCarthy as a defiant seditionist was added the image of McCarthy as a burly, bare-knuckled fighter—a man outside the rules of decent behavior on a personal as well as a political level. His constant interruptions ("A point of order, Mr. Chairman. A point of order!"), his open contempt for his fellow senators (he called Senator Stuart Symington "Sanctimonious Stu," and accused Senator John McClellan of trying to "railroad me to jail"), and his obvious criminality (he had shown himself guilty of sedition, contempt, perjury and faking evidence during the hearings) all made a deep impression on spectators in the Senate Caucus Room and throughout the nation. By the time the hearings were a few weeks old, the crowd of onlookers and reporters in the Caucus Room applauded loudly when Senator Symington, insulted again by McCarthy, declared: "You said something about being afraid. I want you to know from the bottom of my heart that I am not afraid of anything about you or anything you've got to say anytime, anyplace, anywhere!"

But perhaps the most dramatic moments of all were those in which McCarthy, using his favorite tactic of slander, displaying his total amorality, clashed with the noble Joseph Welch, a man committed to an older morality, a more acceptable sense of ethics. It was during the cross-examination of Roy Cohn by Welch that McCarthy, losing all restraint, displayed to the entire nation the essential brutality of his methods.

Roy Cohn in the witness chair (he acted as his own attorney, announcing grandiloquently, "Roy Cohn is here speaking for Roy Cohn to give the facts") was squirming before the gentle persistence of the Boston lawyer. Welch had pointed out that the "information" on which Cohn and McCarthy based their Fort Monmouth investigation had been in their possession for months. Yet they had at no time warned either the army or the FBI about the supposed grave espionage situation there.

WELCH: And on September 7 when you met him [Secretary Stevens] you had in your bosom this alarming situation about Monmouth, is that right?

COHN: Yes, I knew about Monmouth then; yes, sir.

WELCH: And you didn't tug at his lapel and say, "Mr. Secretary, I know something about Monmouth that won't let me sleep nights"?

COHN: I don't know.

WELCH: You didn't do it, did you?

. . . .

WELCH: Have you, did you have, any reason to doubt his [Secretary Stevens's] fidelity?

COHN: No, sir.

WELCH: Or his honor?

COHN: No, sir.

WELCH: Or his patriotism?

COHN: No, sir.

WELCH: And yet, Mr. Cohn, you didn't tell him what you knew?

COHN: I don't remember. . . .

. . . .

WELCH: May I add my small voice, sir, and say whenever you know about a subversive or a Communist or a spy, please hurry. Will you remember these words?

This exchange was too much for Joe McCarthy. Despite Roy Cohn's silently shaking head (one could almost see his lips silently forming the word "No!"), McCarthy charged forward, a big grin on his face to declare: ". . . In view of Mr. Welch's request that the information be given—what we know of anyone who might be performing any work for the Communist party—I think we should tell him that he has in his law firm a young man named Fisher whom he recommended, incidentally, to do the work on this committee, who has been for a number of years a member of an organization which was named—oh, years and years ago—as the legal bulwark of the Communist Party. . . ." The organization, as it turned out, was the National Lawyers Guild, and it had been labeled a "red front" by the House Un-American Activities Committee.

"Now I'm not asking you at this time," McCarthy roared on, "why you tried to force him on this committee. That you did, the committee knows. Whether you knew he was a member of that Communist organization or not I don't know. I assume you did not, Mr. Welch, because I get the impression that while you are quite an actor, you play for a laugh. I don't think you have any conception of the danger of the Communist Party. I don't think you yourself would ever knowingly aid the communist cause. I think you're unknowingly aiding it when you try to burlesque this hearing in which we are attempting to bring out the facts. . . ."

Chairman Karl Mundt broke into this harangue to state: "The Chair wishes to say that he has no recognition or no memory of Mr. Welch recommending Mr. Fisher or anybody else as counsel for this committee."

Having thus been called a liar to his face, Senator McCarthy walked over to his staff table, muttering something to the effect that he would show a news story clipped from some newspaper which would prove his point.

All this time Joseph Welch stared in stunned silence at McCarthy, his face growing livid with rage. Finally he spoke, and his voice quivered: "Senator McCarthy, I did not know, Senator," he called to McCarthy, whose back was turned toward him, "Senator . . . Senator, sometimes you say 'May I have your attention.' May I have yours, Senator?"

McCarthy, looking through newspaper clippings at his staff table, replied: "I'm listening to someone in one ear and you in the other."

"Now this time, sir, I want you to listen with both!"

"Yes, sir," McCarthy replied indifferently.

"Senator, you won't need anything in the record when I finish telling you this," Welch persisted, tears clouding his eyes. "Until this moment, Senator, I think I never really gauged your cruelty or your recklessness.

"Fred Fisher is a young man who went to Harvard Law School and came into my firm and is starting what looks to be a brilliant career with us. When I decided to work for this committee I asked Jim St. Clair, who sits on my right, to be my first assistant. I said to him: 'Jim, pick somebody in the firm to work under you that you would like.'

"He chose Fred Fisher and they came down [to Washington] on an afternoon plane. That night when we had taken a little stab at trying to see what the case was all about, Fred Fisher and Jim St. Clair and I went to dinner together.

"I then said to these young men: 'Boys, I don't know anything about you except I've always liked you, but if there's anything funny in the life of either one of you that would hurt anybody in this case, you had better speak up quick.'

"And Fred Fisher said: 'Mr. Welch, when I was in law school

and for a period of months after, I belonged to the Lawyers Guild,' as you have suggested, Senator.

"He went on to say, 'I am the secretary of the Young Republicans League with the son of the Massachusetts governor and I have the respect and admiration of my community and I'm sure I have the respect and admiration of the twenty-five lawyers or so in Hale and Dorr.'

"And I said, 'Fred, I just don't think I'm going to ask you to work on this case. If I do, one of these days that will come out and go over national television and it will hurt like the dickens.'

"So, Senator, I asked him to go back to Boston. Little did I dream that you could be so reckless and so cruel as to do an injury to that lad. It is true he is still with Hale and Dorr. It is true that he will continue to be with Hale and Dorr.

"It is, I regret to say, equally true that I fear he shall always bear a scar, needlessly inflicted by you. If it were in my power to forgive you for your reckless cruelty, I would do so. I like to think I'm a gentle man, but your forgiveness will have to come from someone other than me."

McCarthy, seemingly unaware of the ominous hush that had fallen over the Caucus Room, rustled some papers and attempted to carry on. He said that Welch "has been baiting Mr. Cohn here for hours. I just wanted to give this man's record. . . ."

"Senator," Welch cut in icily, "may we not drop this? We know he belonged to the Lawyers Guild."

"Let me finish this!" McCarthy shouted.

"And Mr. Cohn nods his head at me," Welch continued. "I did you, I think, no personal injury, Mr. Cohn?"

"No, sir," Roy Cohn affirmed.

"I meant to do you no personal injury, and if I did, I beg your pardon. Let us not assassinate this lad further, Senator. You've done enough. Have you no sense of decency, sir? At long last, have you left no sense of decency?"

McCarthy attempted to carry on, until finally Welch said: "Mr. McCarthy, I will not discuss this further with you. You have sat within six feet of me and could ask, could have asked me about Fred Fisher. You have seen fit to bring it out, and if there is a God in Heaven it will do neither you nor your cause any good.

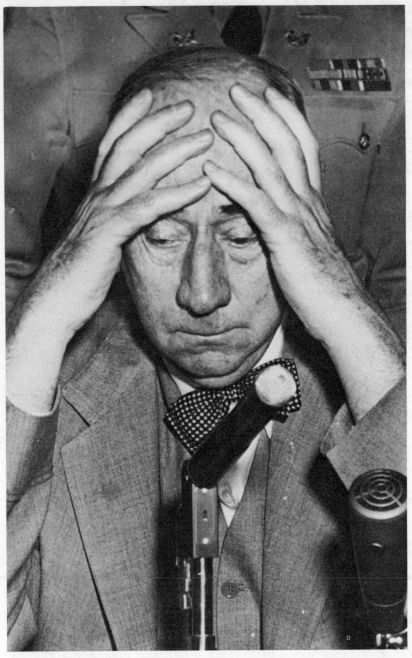

Army counsel Joseph Nye Welch a few moments after his bitter denunciation of Joe McCarthy at the Army-McCarthy hearings. Visibly shaken by his ordeal, the Boston lawyer seems to be pondering the fate of a nation that elevates men like McCarthy to national power.

"I will not discuss it further. I will not ask Mr. Cohn any more questions. You, Mr. Chairman, may, if you will, call the next witness."

For a full minute the Caucus Room was enveloped in complete silence. Then suddenly the silence gave way to thunderous applause. Senators, investigators, lawyers, spectators, reporters, cameramen—all joined in cheering Joseph Nye Welch. Chairman Karl Mundt could not control this spontaneous outburst. When it ended he merely called for a five-minute recess.

Through it all Senator Joseph R. McCarthy had sat slumped in his chair, his face flushed. As those in the Caucus Room brushed past him, ignoring him, drawing back from his presence as they might from that of a leper, Tail-Gunner Joe could only spread his hands and mumble plaintively: "What did I do wrong?"

And so the hearings continued for thirty-six days. The picture they created in the public mind was not only extremely damaging to Joe McCarthy; it was also damaging to the entire Eisenhower administration. For it was soon clear that Secretary of the Army Robert Stevens had been a victim of the administration's timidity before McCarthyism. Here was the secretary of the army obviously trying to placate a playboy like G. David Schine and an unsavory opportunist like Roy Cohn. Here was the Pentagon quailing before the hot air emitted by Joe McCarthy. Here were highly placed public servants engaged in appeasing at any price a cheap demagogue. And the reason they did it was simply that they knew they would receive no support from the White House if they attempted to stand up against McCarthyism. Why would they receive no support? For two prime reasons. First of all, the Republican Party, having made its own use of McCarthy and his tactics, felt it could not politically afford to expose (i.e., destroy) him. And Dwight D. Eisenhower was nothing if not a loyal Party man. Secondly, it was true that the president felt it beneath his dignity to "get in the gutter" with McCarthy and slug it out. He felt it beneath his personal dignity and, more importantly, beneath the dignity of his high office. Of course, in the long run, he had been forced to take a stand in support of his own army secretary, but all through the hearings, as for so many months before them, the White House maintained a studied silence.

167

On August 31, 1954, having listened to more than two million words of testimony, the permanent subcommittee issued its reports to the Senate. The Republican majority report concluded that the charges brought by McCarthy against the army were unfounded, and they were summarily dismissed. On the other hand, the Republican report criticized Secretary Stevens for "placation, appeasement and vacillation." The secretary, the Republican senators concluded, should have dismissed Roy Cohn's endeavors on behalf of G. David Schine immediately, firmly and finally. As for the army charges against McCarthy and Cohn, the Republican report found that Senator McCarthy had not been "personally involved" in Cohn's activities on behalf of Schine. But it criticized the senator for not exercising tighter control over his staff to prevent them from trying to suborn the army on behalf of Schine. Furthermore, the Republicans found that Roy Cohn had indeed been "unduly aggressive" in his efforts to help his friend. But the Republicans could find no evidence that Cohn had attempted to blackmail the army through the Fort Monmouth investigations.

The Democratic minority report was, of course, far more critical of McCarthy and Cohn. Like their Republican colleagues they dismissed McCarthy's charges against the army. But unlike their committee co-members they found that Roy Cohn "misused and abused the powers of his office" in attempting to help Schine. They found, too, that Senator McCarthy had known all about it and had condoned it. "For these inexcusable actions Senator McCarthy and Mr. Cohn merit severe criticism," the Democrats declared.

As for the contradictions in evidence produced during the McCarthy-Cohn-Army hearings, the matter of the faked photograph, of the stolen FBI letter, of the many inexplicable lapses of memory suffered by McCarthy's staff during the proceedings—both the Republican and the Democratic reports urged that all of this be investigated by the Justice Department with a view to prosecuting the guilty. Such prosecutions, of course, were never instituted.

But they were hardly necessary in any case. Roy Cohn had been destroyed by the hearings; his usefulness to McCarthy was ended, and he was persona non grata everywhere in Washington. He accordingly resigned from the permanent subcommittee staff and retired into the comfortable obscurity of a business career in New

York. G. David Schine returned to his army post. Joseph Nye Welch went back to Boston (and later developed his acting talents into a brief motion-picture career). And Senator Joseph Raymond McCarthy? Well, the hearings were over and he was still around. He had survived many another Senate investigation, and it looked as though he might survive this one as well. The public memory is short, after all, and easily distracted. Already Tail-Gunner Joe was speaking ominously of investigations into the CIA, the defense industries, and—yes, the army. But in all of this Joe McCarthy was simply whistling in the dark. For quite apart from the army hearings, the junior senator from Wisconsin had been offered a mortal challenge by one of his Senate colleagues.

CHAPTER TEN

The Toboggan

He [McCarthy] dons his warpaint. He goes into his war
dance. He emits his warwhoops. He goes forth to battle
and proudly returns with the scalp of a pink army
dentist. We may assume that this represents the depth
and seriousness of Communist penetration at this time.

—SEN. RALPH E. FLANDERS (R., VT.)

SOME TIME before the army hearings came to an end (indeed, eight
days before Joseph Nye Welch speared McCarthy on the harpoon
of his righteous indignation), Senator Ralph E. Flanders, the
distinguished seventy-three-year-old Republican senator from the
Green Mountain State, long a foe of McCarthy, feeling that his own
and the Senate's honor had been sufficiently outraged by the antics
of Tail-Gunner Joe, arose on the Senate floor and denounced him.
He labeled McCarthy an adult "Dennis the Menace" and pointed
out that McCarthy's anticommunism "completely parallels that of
Adolf Hitler."

But Senator Flanders found, as had many before him, that
somehow the press and radio were not very much interested in
speeches denouncing McCarthy. Neither, it seemed, were his
Senate colleagues. The aged parliamentarian took thought. How to
get his message before the public? How to force the Senate to act?
Then he had an inspiration. Just a few dozen yards from the Senate
floor, the most publicized hearings in American history were being
held. They were being watched on TV by many millions of
Americans. A challenge delivered there could not possibly be
ignored. Accordingly, on the morning of June 11, Flanders stalked
down the corridors to the Caucus Room.

"So I entered the big hearing room," he later recalled, "and began to look about for a clear way to the witness table where the senator [McCarthy] was testifying. Immediately the reporters sensed that something unusual was in the air, and voices saying 'this way—this way' came to my ear. The hot blast from the lights and the eyes of the television cameras were pointed my way. I reached the table and handed this letter to the senator, which he read aloud:

" 'This is to inform you that I plan to make another speech concerning your activities in the Senate this afternoon as soon after the morning hour as I can get the floor.

" 'If you desire, I will be glad to have you present.' "

In the face of this publicly delivered challenge there was no possible retreat, nor could the mass media now ignore Flanders's attack. And Flanders kept his promise. On the afternoon of June 11, 1954, he introduced Senate Resolution 261: "Resolved, That the conduct of the senator from Wisconsin is unbecoming a member of the United States Senate, is contrary to senatorial traditions, and tends to bring the Senate into disrepute, and such conduct is hereby condemned."

Now the gauntlet of battle had truly been thrown down. But it seemed that few of Senator Flanders's colleagues were eager to seize it. Neither, for that matter, was the Eisenhower administration. Intense pressure was brought upon Flanders by leading members of the administration to withdraw his resolution. He stoutly refused, and as a result a three-day debate ensued on the Senate floor. McCarthy's old cronies rushed to his defense. Senate Republican Majority Leader William F. Knowland (from California and the China Lobby) managed to prevent an immediate vote on the resolution. Silver-maned syntax strangler Everett McKinley Dirksen of Illinois said: "The senator from Vermont and the *Daily Worker* are on the same side of this issue." Senator Homer Capehart of Indiana declared that the Flanders resolution was "an attack on the Congress of the United States." And Tail-Gunner Joe himself sneered that Flanders was "senile" and added; "I think they should get a man with a net and take him to a good, quiet place."

Yet the public wrath generated by Ed Murrow's television show and by the army hearings was such that the Senate could not avoid

Republican Senator Ralph Flanders of Vermont, whose rock-ribbed conscience could no longer tolerate McCarthy's antics, finally forced the Senate to face its responsibilities.

the issue. The best that Majority Leader Knowland could do for his friend was to prevent an immediate vote of censure by once again appointing a committee to investigate McCarthy's behavior. This was to be a select committee of six senators (three Republicans and three Democrats). The Senate voted overwhelmingly in favor of Knowland's proposal (75 to 12), mainly because they expected such an investigation to result in a quiet burial of the entire matter. In this, however, they were mistaken.

Since no senator wanted to cross the man who had presumably destroyed the careers of such men as Scott Lucas, Millard Tydings, and William Benton, those who were to serve on the select committee had to be drafted. The committee was composed of senators who had remained neutral regarding McCarthyism. The chairman of the select committee was Senator Arthur V. Watkins, Republican from Utah. His Republican colleagues included Frank Carlson of Kansas and Francis Case of South Dakota. The Democratic senators joining them were Samuel J. Ervin, Jr., of North Carolina, Edwin C. Johnson of Colorado and John C. Stennis of Mississippi. On the whole, it was a conservative collection.

And yet, one of the most significant points about McCarthy's Senate career was that he had not only outraged liberal Senators; his wild-swinging attacks on *any* Senate member and on such men as George C. Marshall had earned him the enmity of even the most conservative senators, as he was now to learn.

An example of how McCarthy's pigeons were now coming home to roost may be seen in the activities of Missouri's Democratic Senator Thomas C. Hennings. A mild-spoken, courteous man whose conservative views endeared him to the southern or "stone age" wing of his own party, Tom Hennings, as one of his colleagues put it, "didn't come to Washington fighting anybody." But Hennings had had the misfortune to be assigned to that long-ago Gillette subcommittee which investigated McCarthy's share in the corrupt election campaign that unseated Maryland Senator Millard Tydings. Merely because of his assignment to this subcommittee (and before it had issued any report) McCarthy had taxed Hennings with the fact that one of his law partners had once undertaken to act as counsel for an accused Communist leader.

This had led Hennings to reproach McCarthy on the Senate floor, yet it did not at that time lead to Hennings's enlistment in the small anti-McCarthy camp. Later, in 1952, Hennings served on the second Gillette subcommittee, the one that heard Senator Benton's charges of corruption against McCarthy. McCarthy's contemptuous refusal to so much as appear before this second subcommittee had seriously disturbed and angered Hennings, who was more likely to be concerned by senatorial propriety than by the pros or cons of "McCarthyism." When many of his co-members on that subcommittee (including its chairman, Guy Gillette), in their growing fear of McCarthy, had either absented themselves or resigned, Tom Hennings had found himself in de facto charge of its proceedings. The subcommittee report was generally known as the "Hennings report." In all conscience, it was mild enough. In spite of overwhelming evidence of financially corrupt activities, it made no specific recommendations for senatorial action against McCarthy. Tail-Gunner Joe immediately lashed out at Hennings as a "left-winger" and a "lackey" for the Truman administration.

McCarthy, whose political life lay outside the "inner club" of the Senate, might dismiss the Hennings report as "propaganda." But actually it was a carefully considered document addressed primarily to fellow senators. Now, two years later, with the Flanders Resolution evoking yet another investigation of the junior senator from Wisconsin, quiet Tom Hennings made it his business to remind his colleagues of the way in which McCarthy had insulted and obstructed senatorial processes in the past with impunity. The fact that these promptings came from so stalwart a conservative as Hennings lent them very great weight with those Southern Democrats who had not been opposed to "McCarthyism" as such on principle. Many of them evidently reasoned that if over the years, McCarthy could rouse the very real enmity of a man like Tom Hennings, it might be time to call a halt.

Flanders's charges against McCarthy were grouped by the select committee into five main categories: his contemptuous conduct toward the Gillette committee; his appeal to federal employees to become seditionists by supplying him with classified government documents; his use of such classified documents; his insulting behavior toward senators Hendrickson and Flanders; and his behavior toward General Zwicker.

The select committee hearings were held in that same Senate Caucus Room so recently the stage of the McCarthy-Cohn-Army drama. But this time television and newsreel cameras were banned. Chairman Watkins was determined to prevent the hearings from degenerating into a publicity circus. He was also determined that the hearings would not be confused or led astray by the rantings of McCarthy. On the very first day, when McCarthy tried to obfuscate matters by attacking one of the select committee members, Watkins banged down his gavel.

WATKINS: The senator is out of order. (*bang*)

McCARTHY: Can't I get the senator to tell me—

WATKINS: The senator is out of order. (*bang*)

McCARTHY: —whether it is true or false?

WATKINS: The senator is out of order. (*bang*) . . . We are not going to be diverted by these diversions and sidelines.

There was no question after this exchange as to who was going to run the hearings, or how tightly they would focus upon McCarthy himself. Having been badly bruised at the army hearings, Tail-Gunner Joe now decided to calm down and follow the advice of his own attorney, Edward Bennett Williams, who had agreed to help him only on the condition that McCarthy would follow his instructions.

Williams made the only possible defense under the circumstances—that what McCarthy had done, others had done. McCarthy's treatment of Zwicker, for example: just a few days earlier Senator Prescott Bush of Connecticut had been accused of similar mistreatment of witnesses while conducting a one-man hearing on the subject of public housing. As for McCarthy giving out classified information, was it not true that Senator Edwin Johnson, a member of this very select committee, had a few years ago uttered classified information about the hydrogen bomb over national television? It was true that McCarthy had called Senator Flanders "senile." But Flanders had compared McCarthy to Hitler. Which was more insulting? It was also true that McCarthy had asked federal employees to give him classified information, but Senator Watkins

The Watkins committee completes its report on the motion to censure McCarthy. Seated around the table from left to right: Senators Frank Carlson (R., Kan.); John C. Stennis (D., Miss.); Arthur C. Watkins (R., Utah), chairman; Edwin C. Johnson (R., Colo.); Francis Case (R., S.D.); and Sam Ervin (D., N.C.).

himself had recently signed a committee report in which it was urged that "employees of the executive branch . . . turn over to committees of Congress any information which would help the committees in their fight against subversion." In other words, if Senator Joseph R. McCarthy was to be censured or condemned for these activities, then many other members of the Senate should likewise be censured or condemned.

Of course all of this overlooked the central point, which was McCarthy's conduct considered in its entirety. What some senators did once in their careers, he did constantly; what some senators did by mistake, he did intentionally. But for the select committee to have considered McCarthy's career in its entirety would have led to a serious embarrassment. For they could not possibly fail to condemn and censure that entire career without leaving themselves and the Senate open to a fatal question: why had they not censured and condemned McCarthy and his tactics years ago?

In the end, the select committee reported that Senator Joseph R.

McCarthy ought to be censured on two counts: his contempt of the Gillette committee and his behavior toward General Zwicker. The other charges were dropped, mainly because of the persuasive arguments of attorney Edward Bennett Williams. Senate debate on the select committee's report and recommendations opened on November 10, 1954, and was to continue for more than a week.

Free from the restraining advice of his attorney, McCarthy now resorted to his familiar tactics. In the Senate and on national television he attacked the select committee itself. He accused some of its members of "deliberate deception" and others of "fraud." He declared that the hearings had been a "lynching bee" and that Chairman Watkins was "stupid." The select committee, he ranted, had been the "unwitting handmaiden" and "the attorneys in fact of the Communist Party." McCarthy's supporters throughout the country mobilized to "save Joe."

A group calling itself "Ten Million Americans Mobilizing for Justice" came into being, led by such McCarthyites as Lieutenant General George E. Stratemeyer, ex-air force commander; Admiral William H. Standley, ex-chief of naval operations; Charles Edison, ex-secretary of the navy; General James A. Van Fleet, ex-Eighth Army commander in Korea, among many other "ex's." And of course they were joined by such as the Daughters of the American Revolution, the Daughters of I Shall Return, etc., etc. The group was actually able to find slightly more than one million signatures for a petition in support of McCarthy—and nearly one thousand people to descend personally on Washington bearing objects like nets to snare Senator Flanders and placards demanding "Who Promoted Peress?"

The Senate debate was hot. McCarthy's supporters took the line that in voting to censure or condemn Joe McCarthy, the Senate would be giving ground to communism. If McCarthy was censured, cried Senator Herman Welker, Red China would soon be admitted into the United Nations. If McCarthy fell, Senator Barry Goldwater of Arizona declared, then FBI head J. Edgar Hoover would be the next to go.

But Senator Watkins was having none of this. "I am asking all of my colleagues in the Senate," he said, "—and it must be remembered that we members of the select committee were practically drafted for the job, and so far as I am concerned it was the most unpleasant task I have ever had to perform in my public life—I am asking all my colleagues, 'What are you going to do about it?'

"That is what I want to know. That is what all members of the select committee want to know from all senators. . . ."

This was an appeal that very few senators could resist. Each of them knew that at any time they too could be drafted to serve on such a select committee. In effect, Watkins was demanding that the Senate either accept the select committee's report or vote to condemn itself.

Faced with this choice, the Senate grudgingly acted. It changed the terms of the resolution, retaining the select committee's first count regarding McCarthy's contempt of the Gillette committee, but dropping the second count regarding his conduct toward General Zwicker. For this second count it substituted a new charge based on McCarthy's attacks on the select committee itself. Then finally, on December 2, 1954, the United States Senate took the step it could have taken months and years before; it voted that "the conduct of the senator from Wisconsin, Mr. McCarthy, is contrary to senatorial traditions . . . tended to bring the Senate into dishonor and disrepute, to obstruct the constitutional processes of the Senate, and to impair its dignity; and such conduct is hereby condemned."

The vote in favor of condemnation was 67 to 22. Those senators who showed themselves McCarthyites to the bitter end included Barry Goldwater of Arizona, Karl Mundt of South Dakota, Roman L. Hruska of Nebraska, Styles Bridges of New Hampshire, Everett McKinley Dirksen of Illinois, William F. Knowland of California, Herman Welker of Idaho and Homer Capehart of Indiana—all Republicans.

And so Senator Joseph R. McCarthy stood "condemned" by the Senate. And so what? he might have said; he was still a United States senator. He still sat on the same Senate committees. He still retained throughout the nation his hordes of true believers. He had been rebuked by his colleagues. What did that mean to a man who throughout his entire career had kept out of the "establishment," indeed made a career of attacking it? Would this Senate action undermine his political base in Wisconsin, and would Wisconsin voters be ashamed to return to the Senate a man condemned by that body? There was no reason to think so. Joe McCarthy's Senate seat was safe until 1956, sufficient time for him to recapture the initiative while his constituents forgot about Senate condemnation.

But, amazingly, Joe McCarthy did not say, "So what?" Something in him broke on December 2, 1954, and was never repaired. As suddenly as it had started just a few years before, his career came to an end—his career as a demagogue, that is. All the wind seemed to have been knocked out of him. "I wouldn't exactly call it a vote of confidence," McCarthy said on December 2, "but I don't feel I've been lynched." What did it matter then that the Gallup Poll showed that 36 percent of all Americans were still for him, even after condemnation? What did it matter if 13,000 screaming fanatics mobilized by the Committee of Ten Million turned out in Madison Square Garden, New York, to roar their support for Tail-Gunner Joe? McCarthy did not attend that rally; he was at Bethesda Naval Hospital outside Washington being treated for an injured arm. Somehow or other Joe McCarthy knew that he was beaten. Since he rarely thought deeply about anything, it is improbable that he ever analyzed the reasons for his defeat. But certain factors seem incontestable.

The most important of these was, obviously, that the Senate in its majority had at long last shown itself unafraid of McCarthy politically. In other words, those sixty-seven Senators who voted to condemn McCarthy, having tested the political air, had decided that it was now safe to oppose Tail-Gunner Joe; he could do them no real harm at home. And without fear as his whip in dealing with the Senate, McCarthy could count on no further victories there. He had always been detested by the liberal bloc of senators; and after his attack on George C. Marshall he had earned the enmity of the southern bloc. His attack on the Watkins Select Committee had finally stirred the wrath of Republican conservatives. No one was going to listen to him again in the Senate or before Senate committees.

The strength of the Senate revulsion was a reflection of new political realities. For the Democrats (who had just regained control of Congress in the 1954 midterm elections) it was an all-or-nothing decision. The uses of the Menace, especially as represented by its master propagator, threatened to split and thus destroy the Democratic Party. Somewhere along the line the Party would have to make a stand. That it did so as late as December 1954 (and then uncertainly) speaks volumes about the distinct fear the Democrats had entertained of Joe McCarthy. And it must always be remembered that this fear was compounded by the fact that citizens could always be accused, not merely of attacking the man who attacked the Reds, but also of attacking him for purely partisan reasons—because he was a Republican. Thus the Democrats felt themselves bound to wait for Republican initiative when it came to dealing with the Republican senator from Wisconsin.

That this Republican initiative was finally forthcoming reflected a second new political reality—the popularity of Dwight D. Eisenhower as president. Perhaps, in a minor way, Walter Lippmann was right. Perhaps the fact that after so many decades of Democratic presidents the Republicans finally won the White House did serve to modify the Republican desperation that was willing to make use of McCarthy. Once Eisenhower himself decided to throw his political weight against McCarthy, the issue could no longer be in doubt. That he waited so long to do so reflected not simply his personal distaste for such combat, but also his misconception of the office of the presidency. Eisenhower conceived his position akin to that of a chairman of the board. His subordinates were to manage the government while he presided, keeping them happy, reminding them from time to time of their duty, resolving their conflicts. It was thus he had managed the Allied generals under his command during the war in Europe, and thus he had attended to the affairs of Columbia University after the war. But the presidency is not comparable to the office of chairman of the board. It is above all a position of moral leadership. Without such leadership, vigorously exercised, a vacuum is created. Into that vacuum rush all the regional, special and private fears, ambitions and interests of a complex society. Only the president speaks for the nation as a whole; only the president represents *all* the people (even those who voted against him) in our government. By rejecting this position of national moral leadership, Dwight D. Eisenhower left the field to those "political plungers" (as Adlai Stevenson called them) who would use, or suffer the use of, any means to attain their private ends. But once Eisenhower spoke up against McCarthy (however belatedly and reluctantly), the people responded.

And yet none of these objective reasons seems sufficient to explain the sudden fall of Joe McCarthy. He was a demagogue *par excellence,* a medicine man from the piney woods of the West selling his own personal nostrum. But he was by no means a fanatic; on the contrary, he was a cynic. The evidence was overwhelming that he cared not a straw in his heart of hearts about the Menace. To be a fanatic it is necessary to *believe,* and Tail-Gunner Joe never believed in much of anything except his own well-being. He was able to rouse true fanatics because he had caught the rhythms and tone of the incantations they liked to hear. But he uttered them without real conviction. Indeed, his pursuit of "the enemy" had always been haphazard and even half-hearted. As soon as he felt he had reaped as many headlines as any investigation could fertilize, he moved on to other topics. Yet precisely because he was not a fanatic in the mode of, say, Adolf Hitler, but rather a demagogue in the mode of Huey Long, his collapse after 1954 is all the more puzzling. Traditionally, demagogues are fast-moving targets, very resilient, able to bounce back after a defeat. Being outside the establishment, a demagogue is not dependent on its favor or good wishes—and hence is not susceptible to its disciplines. Richard Rovere put the matter succinctly: "McCarthy was finished in 1954 not because he had suffered wounds of a kind no demagogue could survive, but because he had suffered wounds that a particular demagogue named Joseph R. McCarthy could not survive."

McCarthy, as even his bitterest enemies testified, was a hard man not to like on the personal level. He was genial, demonstratively friendly, and always deeply puzzled when those whom he had attacked took personal offense. His gesture at the end of that day during the army hearings when Joseph Welch publicly dissected him—the spreading of the hands, the genuine bewilderment behind the words "What did I do wrong?"—were very real, pathetically real. McCarthy, like many a loudly aggressive individual, lived with deep feelings of inadequacy. He wanted very much to be liked. He wanted very much to be liked by his fellow senators as well as by the public. He had come to Washington from the rough and tumble of graft-ridden local politics in Wisconsin with the conviction that in politics anything goes. He was not far wrong there. But his style, his manner, his very being, insofar as they forced his Senate colleagues to see themselves in a distorted yet very real mirror, offended them and frightened them. In a sense his entire Senate career may be seen as the increasingly desperate attempt of an outcast, a pariah, to establish contact with his fellows.

After 1954 this contact was irrevocably denied to McCarthy, and after that he could never summon the energy to perform. During the last years of his life, when he rose to speak on the Senate floor, his colleagues would drift from the chamber; reporters in the Senate galleries would leave to get a cup of coffee. When on occasion he would wander into some committee hearing, no heads turned, no flash bulbs exploded, no television cameras swiveled. He was no longer news.

He made various half-hearted attempts to find some new political gimmick that would put him back in the headlines. These included such nonsense as his advocating that General Douglas MacArthur be put in charge of all American foreign policy, or his revelation that John Foster Dulles had hired 150 men to censor the records of the Yalta conference. On other occasions he would rise to advocate large increases in the air force appropriation, or some giveaway program for the nation's farmers. But none of these matters provided the raw meat upon which McCarthy flourished. He seemed listless in his advocacy, fatalistic about his future. His political fortunes had fallen to such a low level that he could not even get his personal candidate appointed postmaster in his own hometown of Appleton, Wisconsin.

During the 1956 presidential campaign the Republican Party, which had made such effective use of McCarthy's demagoguery four years before, shunned him. He did not even attend the Republican National Convention that year. Eisenhower was no longer, of course, McCarthy's idea of a good president. He futilely hoped that FBI chief J. Edgar Hoover would be the Republican candidate instead. Eisenhower's reelection left McCarthy cold, as increasingly did the entire political process.

A psychiatrist analyzing McCarthy's behavior in 1954 wrote: ". . . McCarthy is now on a downgrade course. With the resilience of his mental makeup, he is unlikely to become overtly insane. It is more likely that he will become a prey to physical ailments. Alcohol may be used increasingly to allay anxiety. . . . This form of alcoholism, if it should occur, is the desperate type. . . ."

The psychiatrist was right. During the last two and a half years of his life, McCarthy (who had always been a heavy drinker, but by no means an alcoholic) turned increasingly to the bottle for solace. His admissions to Bethesda Naval Hospital to be dried out (always disguised as being for some other physical ailment) grew more and more frequent.

In the spring of 1957 Joe McCarthy seemed, for a moment, to regain some of his energy. He spoke of plans to buy "a little cattle spread" in Arizona to which he hoped to retire with his wife, Gene, and their adopted daughter, Tierney Elyzabeth. For some time he had been devoting himself to the stock market, and he had evidently been quite successful. Then his stocks plunged—and so did Joe. He began drinking furiously again. On April 28, 1957, he was admitted to Bethesda Naval Hospital for the last time. It was given out that he had gone there for treatment of a knee injury. But of course he had gone there to be resurrected from his alcoholic stupor. This time the treatment did not work. McCarthy's liver simply couldn't take any more. He died on May 2, 1957, of "acute hepatitic infection," said the hospital; of cirrhosis of the liver, said insiders.

A memorial service for Senator Joseph R. McCarthy was held in the United States Senate. There the men whose careers he had tried to assassinate, the men who had advanced themselves by adopting his tactics, the men who had feared him, the men who had detested him—all joined in wishing his corpse well. The Senate chaplain, evidently himself prey to fears of the Menace, said: "And so this fallen warrior, though dead, speaketh, calling a nation of freemen to be delivered from the complacency of a false security and from regarding those who loudly sound the trumpets of vigilance and alarm as mere disturbers of the peace."

And so McCarthy was gone, his body interred in Appleton, Wisconsin. But he left behind him a bitter legacy—a legacy which was to endure for years and to affect the nation in many ways which are only now becoming apparent.

All through Joe McCarthy's career the State Department had been his prime target. Whether it was headed by Dean Acheson (the "Red Dean," McCarthy loved to call him) or by the impeccably conservative John Foster Dulles made no difference. McCarthy's assaults drove from the department many if not all of its top far eastern experts (in this sense the China Lobby may be said to have triumphed). It drove out those men whose knowledge and dedication to far eastern affairs might well have prevented the American buildup in Vietnam, for example. Furthermore, the furor raised by McCarthy and his legions made it politically impossible for the American government to carry on any kind of rational policy in regard to Asia. No elected public official of the time could possibly afford to even discuss a rapprochement with Communist China, for instance, or the abandonment of the moribund Chiang Kai-shek regime on Formosa without fear of being hounded from office as a "dupe" at best, a traitor at worst. It may be said that to a very large extent America's tragic war in Vietnam is one part of the legacy of McCarthyism.

The McCarthy method of investigation—the hounding and battering of witnesses before his committee—although not wholly invented by him, was undoubtedly perfected in his hands. And this technique became a favorite method with other congressmen on other committees. Thus it may be said that part of the McCarthy legacy has been the brutalizing of certain congressional procedures. To this day such groups as the House Un-American Activities Committee continue to hound private citizens, not for the purposes of investigation, but in order to slander them before their fellow Americans.

Perhaps the most important and lasting legacy of the days of Joe McCarthy has been the polarizing, the emboldenment of the radical right in America. During the senator's supremacy all the racists, the neo-Fascists reflected his glory, basked in the suddenly respectable publicity of his work. Many Americans, unbalanced by the pressures of living in the dangerous mid-twentieth century, were driven into the arms of these extremist groups. One should never forget that 36 percent of the nation's population "approved" of Tail-Gunner Joe even after he had been censured. These admirers received the news of his death as a personal wound inflicted upon them. Joe McCarthy, they said, had been murdered by the "pinks, punks, and perverts" in Washington. He was a martyr to the cause of 100 percent Americanism—that is to say, political paranoia. Only a few months after his death, the seeds planted during his career began to bloom in such Fascist direct-action organizations as the John Birch Society. Since his death the extreme right has been feverishly arming itself, not with rhetoric this time, but with guns and grenades. The atmosphere of terror he created worked both ways. McCarthy and his legions terrorized decent citizens, but they also terrorized themselves. Joe might have been cynical about it all, but his followers were not. They really believed in the Conspiracy and the Menace—and McCarthy delicately fostered their nightmare fears for his own purposes. These fears, once aroused, were not easy to dampen. They flourish to this day. They were the fears that saturated the city of Dallas, Texas, for example, when President John F. Kennedy fell victim to their direct expression. They are the fears that have made the assassination of public figures almost a common occurrence in recent years.

On the other hand, the reaction against McCarthyism revivified in some Americans a dedication to constitutional principles. Reacting against a decade of repressive legislation and the erosion of basic American rights, the Supreme Court in the years following McCarthy's death declared unconstitutional many of the insane laws passed by a frantic and hag-ridden Congress during the early fifties. In so doing, the Court found occasion not only to preserve those rights assured to all Americans by their nation's Charter, but also to greatly broaden the scope of freedom. It may be said that the reaction of the Supreme Court to the hysteria of McCarthysim actually resulted in greater liberty for more Americans.

Other strange reactions to McCarthyism might be noted. Previously we examined something of the impact of the McCarthy hysteria on universities throughout the land. We went so far as to ascribe to these effects the emergence of what was called the "silent generation" of graduates. The habit of fear induced by McCarthy in the groves of academe died hard. But die it did. And if the climate of fear in the fifties produced the silent generation, the following generations of university students, reacting against the shameful example of their forerunners, were anything but silent.

185

One of the primary aims of the student riots of the sixties was to force professors and college administrators out of their fears, to force them to speak up and to participate in political activities. Without overburdening the chain of cause and effect, it may at least be argued that one of the great reactions to McCarthysim was the atmosphere of radicalism in the academic world of the sixties.

Of course the phenomena about which we have been speculating did not derive solely from the activities of Joseph Raymond McCarthy. The radical right we have with us always; political paranoia is an endemic disease in a democracy; elements of venality and cowardice in public life have long been the norm. All the preconditions for a traumatic postwar hysteria had long been present when Tail-Gunner Joe arrived on the scene. Yet it cannot be denied that he manipulated them artfully. The German philosopher Friedrich Nietzsche, grappling with the problem of the impact of an individual on broad historic events, once wrote: "Here is a hero who did nothing but shake the tree when the fruit was ripe. Do you think that was a small thing to do? Well, just look at the tree he shook."

EPILOGUE

The Nightmare as History

The true theater of a demagogue is a democracy.
—James Fenimore Cooper

From the vantage point of the 1970s, the phenomenon known in its day as McCarthyism seems utterly improbable—even faintly absurd. Were people really suckered into buying that political cure-all by so obvious a humbug? Did adult men and women actually quail before so patent a fraud? To a nation grown used to the most violent and radical kinds of protest, it seems unbelievable that political action and the free expression of ideas ever could have been smothered by such ridiculous bogeymen as the late junior senator from Wisconsin and his hordes. Protest stifled by hysteria? Today it is just the other way around; we stifle our hysteria by protest. And yet the McCarthy saga was true, all too true. To accept that fact is to immediately raise a few interesting questions.

First of all, what basically did McCarthyism represent? We have seen that it was a political device to smash the old New Deal coalition, cunningly employed by certain unscrupulous politicans. We have also seen that it provided an outlet for the paranoia of the lunatic fringe of the extreme right. For its leader it was a means to public notoriety and continued political power. But in the longer perspective of history, what are we to make of it? McCarthyism represented, above all, a flight from reality on the part of the American people—from a reality too complex and bitter to face. It was a distraction from the tensions and fears of the postwar world. Instead of focusing public attention on the very real and deadly threats embodied in that world, it funneled public energies into a mad-hatter's search for shadows under every bed. When this flight from reality was finally absorbed into the deep sleep of the Eisenhower years (another, even more effective means of avoiding reality), its public manifestations subsided.

Could Joe McCarthy ever have seized or won national power? That seems unlikely. As the avowed enemy of the establishment, he could avail himself of none of its means to power. How could he ever have captured the Republican nomination for the presidency, for example? Yet—Barry Goldwater did, didn't he? Still, the engines of political paranoia, fueled as they are by *total* despair, *deep* fright and *intense* hate, moved only a portion of the American electorate during the fifties. The nation would have to undergo trauma on a much grander scale than any it has yet known (including the Civil War) for a dictator to emerge. In this century there have been but two demagogues with anything approaching a national following: Huey Long, the late senator from Louisiana, and Joe Mcarthy. Long's home base was much more securely organized (complete with state troopers playing stormtroopers) than McCarthy's ever was. But in the long run neither man could parlay his local power base into a national one.

For McCarthy to have somehow seized power on a national scale, he would have had to have been a different person. He would have to have had the great faith of the true fanatic. But this pied piper of unreality was far from that. He was, appropriately enough, that most traditional of American figures, the patent medicine salesman from the West. His gaudy wagon arrived in Washington just in time, and for a season or two he kept the nation bemused by his spiel. One can almost hear him now: Step right up, folks! For just one dime, one thin dime, the tenth part of a dollar, take a little swig of ole' Doc McCarthy's remedy for them postwar blues! Brewed by a wild Cherokee medicine man who never told anyone the recipe and died with the secret on his lips! Only a little bit left, so hurry, hurry, hurry. It's nice and shady, it's good for the old lady—there's a baby in every bottle, sir!

Not that this particular medicine man wasn't selling poison. He was, and it would be well not to forget his victims. But when all due reverence has been paid to the damage done by McCarthyism, it still retains that aura of incredible nonsense.

Could it happen again? Are the ingredients still around for another national binge of paranoia?

Well, the paranoid right is still with us. The shadows that trouble its dreams today include not only Communists but also anarchists, hippies, yippies, long-haired people, blacks, the militant poor, etc., etc. And demagogues still rage across the political stage—Spiro Agnew, with McCarthylike attacks on "egghead intellectuals," and his ominous hints about the "conspiracy" of the press, television and radio media; George Wallace of Alabama hoping and praying that someday, somewhere, one of "them pointy-headed, long-haired protesters" will lie down before *his* automobile—"That's the *last* automobile he'll *ever* lie down in front of, folks!"

And of course the scenario of the paranoid nightmare has changed. The lunatic right may still dream of hordes of Russian troops marching down Pennsylvania Avenue, of red flags floating from town post offices, of billions of Red Chinese prodding Americans at bayonet point into reciting the sayings of Chairman Mao, of two hundred million Americans forced to eat nothing but chicken *guy-ding* or hundred-year-old eggs in place of Wheaties, of bewhiskered commissars nationalizing grandmothers and sisters. But this older nightmare has new and disturbing elements that may give it renewed vitality. These new elements include fear of blacks, detestation of the hard-core poor, anxiety at young people who reject traditional values, rage at the new left militancy, unsafe city streets and no doubt much else. But this sick dread of reality which spread across the nation during McCarthy's great days seems today to be limited to the small hard core of incurable right extremists. Perhaps what is lacking is something real and threatening on the international horizon which, when combined with domestic troubles, would be enough to send the majority of sane Americans on another flight from reality. And such a threat can always arise.

So the answer to the question "Can it happen again?" is yes, of course. For, as Ed Murrow pointed out on the television program with which he dissected Joe McCarthy, quoting that mirror of mankind, William Shakespeare: "Cassius was right: 'The fault, dear Brutus, is not in our stars but in ourselves.'"

And as long as we are what we are, the elements of the American nightmare will not disappear; they will only lie dormant in the American mind.

Bibliography

THE MCCARTHY era is so close to our own that much basic research material (such as the private papers of Joseph R. McCarthy) remains unavailable. Much, too, is as yet uncollated—to be unearthed only in newspaper morgues or among back issues of magazines. Nonetheless, for the student who wishes to probe more deeply into the facts, fantasies and passions of those troubled times, the following sources will prove helpful.

For direct research into the several investigations with which Senator McCarthy was associated:

On McCarthy's activities regarding Public Housing:

U.S. Congress, House, 80th Cong., 1st & 2nd sess., Joint Committee on Housing, *Study and Investigation of Housing* (Washington, D.C., 1947–1948)

On McCarthy's intervention in the Malmedy massacre trial:

U.S. Congress, Senate, 81st Cong., 1st sess., Committee on Armed Services, *Malmedy Massacre Investigation* (Washington, D.C., 1949)

On McCarthy's assault on the State Department:

U.S. Congress, Senate, 83rd Cong., 1st sess., Committee on Government Operations, Permanent Subcommittee on Investigations, *State Department—File Survey; State Department Information Program—Voice of America; State Department Information Program—Information Centers; State Department—Student-Teacher Exchange Program; Control of Trade with The Soviet Bloc* (Washington, D.C., 1953)

On McCarthy's assault on the Defense Department:

U.S. Congress, Senate, 83rd Cong., 1st sess., Committee on Government Operations, Permanent Subcommittee on Investigations, *Subversion and Espionage in Defense Establishments and Industry; Army Signal Corps–Subversion and Espionage; Communist Infiltration in the Army* (Washington, D.C., 1953–1954)

The Tydings Committee hearings regarding McCarthy's original charges:

U.S. Congress, Senate, 81st Cong., 2nd sess., Committee on Foreign Relations, *State Department Loyalty Investigation*, Senate Report 2108 (Washington, D.C., 1950)

The Maryland Election Campaign hearings:

U.S. Congress, Senate, 82nd Cong., 1st sess., Committee on Rules and Administration, Subcommittee on Privileges and Elections, *Maryland Senatorial Campaign of 1950*, Senate Report 647 (Washington, D.C., 1950)

Senator Benton's charges against McCarthy:

U.S. Congress, Senate, 82nd Cong., 2nd sess., Committee on Rules and Administration, Subcommittee on Privileges and Elections, *Investigations of Senators Joseph R. McCarthy and William Benton* (Washington, D.C., 1952)

The Army-McCarthy hearings:

U.S. Congress, Senate, 83rd Cong., 2nd sess., Committee on Government Operations, Permanent Subcommittee on Investigations, *Charges and Countercharges Involving Secretary of the Army Robert T. Stevens, John G. Adams, H. Struve Hensel and Senator Joe McCarthy, Roy M. Cohn and Francis P. Carr* (Washington, D.C., 1954)

On the motion to censure McCarthy:

U.S. Congress, Senate, 83rd Cong., 2nd sess., Select Committee to Study Censure Charges, *Report on Resolution to Censure*, Senate Report 2508 (Washington, D.C., 1954)

Secondary material vital to an understanding of the McCarthy phenomenon:

On the general political background from 1932 to 1960:

Agar, Herbert, *The Price of Power: America Since 1945* (Chicago, 1957)

Bell, Daniel (Ed.), *The Radical Right* (New York, 1963)

Donovan, Robert J., *Eisenhower: The Inside Story* (New York, 1956)

Goldman, Eric F., *The Crucial Decade and After: America—1945–1960* (New York, 1961)

Kennan, George F., *Russia and the West Under Lenin and Stalin* (Boston, 1960)

Matthews, Donald, *U. S. Senators and Their World* (Chapel Hill, N.C., 1960)

Maze, Earl, *Richard Nixon: A Political and Personal Portrait* (New York, 1959)

Schlesinger, Arthur M., Jr., *The Age of Roosevelt* (Vols. 1–3) (Cambridge, Mass., 1957–1960)

Truman, Harry S, *Memoirs* (Vols. 1–2) (New York, 1955–1956)

Westerfield, Bradford H., *Foreign Policy and Party Politics* (New Haven, Conn., 1955)

On the Menace and its uses:

Carr, Robert K., *The House Committee on Un-American Activities, 1945–1950* (Ithaca, N.Y., 1952)

Caughey, John W., *In Clear and Present Danger: The Crucial State of Our Freedoms* (Chicago, 1958)

Commager, Henry S., *Freedom, Loyalty and Dissent* (New York, 1954)

Cushman, Robert E., *Civil Liberties in the United States* (Ithaca, N.Y., 1956)

Forster, Arnold, and Epstein, Benjamin R., *The Troublemakers* (New York, 1952)

Goodman, Walter, *The Committee* (New York, 1968)

Harper, Alan D., *The Politics of Loyalty: The White House and the Communist Issue, 1946–1952* (New York, 1969)

Latham, Earl, *The Communist Controversy in Washington: From the New Deal to McCarthy* (Cambridge, Mass., 1966)

Packer, Herbert L., *Ex-Communist Witnesses* (Stanford, Cal., 1962)

Rogin, Michael P., *The Intellectuals and McCarthy: The Radical Specter* (Cambridge, Mass., 1967)

Taylor, Telford, *Grand Inquest: The Story of Congressional Investigations* (New York, 1955)

Memoirs of those involved in aiding or opposing the Menace:

Arnold, Thurmond, *Fair Fights and Foul: A Dissenting Lawyer's Life* (New York, 1965)

Chambers, Whittaker, *Witness* (New York, 1952)

Cooke, Alistair, *A Generation on Trial: USA v. Alger Hiss* (New York, 1950)

Lattimore, Owen, *Ordeal by Slander* (Boston, 1950)

Matusow, Harvey, *False Witness* (New York, 1955)

Straight, Michael, *Trial by Television* (Boston, 1954)

Wechsler, James A., *The Age of Suspicion* (New York, 1953)

On Joseph R. McCarthy and "McCarthyism":

Anderson, Jack, and May, Ronald, *McCarthy: The Man, the Senator, the "Ism"* (Boston, 1952)

Buckley, William F., Jr., and Bozell, L. Brent, *McCarthy and His Enemies: The Record and Its Meaning* (Chicago, 1954)

Cooke, Fred J., *The Nightmare Decade* (New York, 1971)

Griffith, Robert, *The Politics of Fear: Joseph R. McCarthy and the Senate* (Lexington, Ky., 1970)

McCarthy, Joseph R., *McCarthyism: The Fight for America* (New York, 1952)

Rovere, Richard H., *Senator Joe McCarthy* (New York, 1959)

Rubin, Morris, *The McCarthy Record* (Madison, Wis., 1952)

Suggested Reading:

Latham, Earl, *The Communist Controversy in Washington: From the New Deal to McCarthy* (Cambridge, Mass., 1966)

—A broad and intelligent survey of the political uses made of the Menace for the past three generations.

Lattimore, Owen, *Ordeal by Slander* (Boston, 1950)

—How it felt to be one of the victims.

Straight, Michael, *Trial by Television* (Boston, 1954)

—The best account of the Army-McCarthy hearings.

Cooke, Fred J., *The Nightmare Decade* (New York, 1971)

—Gives a detailed picture not only of McCarthy but also of the background and effects of McCarthyism.

Buckley, William F., Jr., and Bozell, L. Brent, *McCarthy and His Enemies: The Record and Its Meaning* (Chicago, 1954)

—A desperate attempt to make McCarthyism intellectually "respectable"; recommended here only because it is one of the very few pro-McCarthy books with any pretense to political or literary dignity.

Rovere, Richard H., *Senator Joe McCarthy* (New York, 1959)

—Written gracefully by a famous Washington correspondent who knew McCarthy personally. This book remains a classic on the subject.

Index